Praise for Heart-Leadership

"You are such an inspiration of action! I loved reading your book it was so you – full of generous, wonderful wisdom. Two sentences I am holding on to are "your heart knows" and also "one-of-a-kind human being". Such beautiful words to anchor in."
Jacquie Landeman, New Zealand Finance Ltd trading as Grabaloan

"Timely. An essential guide to what we all need right now - in business and in life."
Geoff McDonald, Ideas Architect

"Ian Berry is an expert in Heart-Leadership which is handy for all of us. There is a change happening in the way effective leaders work. This book will help you to lead this change and to be your best effective self."
Peter Hills, Group Chairman at Vistage UK

"I loved every page of what you have written."
Rosemary McKenzie-Ferguson, Founder Craig's Table.

"I love your approach and focus and think this is an extremely thoughtful, well written book."
Peter Acheson, Chief Executive Officer, Chandler Macleod Group.

"Ian Berry has produced an important and ground-breaking work which is a crucial addition to our knowledge of leadership and how better leadership can improve all our communities.

This is a transformational work and I cannot recommend it highly enough for leaders wishing to shape a better future."
John F. Kennedy BSc FIDM CMO/Chief Strategist/Digital & Data Science Marketing

"In work and in life, you have an inner 'knowing' of what is right, how to lead, how to nurture to achieve the best for yourself, and other people. Heart-Leadership gives words to that 'knowing' and helps you to articulate what you know, and to share it in your own best way."
Dr. Simone Boer, A/Manager Leisure and Recreation Services City of Greater Geelong

"Ian shares from his own broad experiences, and the inspiring stories of others, the valuable lessons he has learned along the way; that listening to the heart before the head is a first step towards a new kind of leadership... a heart leadership that is so needed in our world after 2020!"
Paul Schmeja, CEO, First Contact

"I've been privileged to be a member of the peer groups that have workshopped Ian's last three books including this one. I've learned that leading from my heart, speaking from my heart, and then letting my head and hands drive the outcomes is an awesome way to live and to lead."
Jamie Wilson Victorian Regional Sales Manager, Haymes Paint

"Without Heart-Leadership there is no real leadership. This is a book – a pathway – a necessity - for our time."
Glenn Capelli CSP Sir Winston Churchill Fellow

"Meeting and working with Ian has completely changed my perspective on leadership. Appreciating people, enhancing their gifts and thinking in possibility are some of the changes he has taught me. Ian has had a significant impact on how I approach by work. His Heart-Leadership book is the next best thing to working with Ian."
Donovan Ryan, IT Manager

Heart-Leadership

Become
the wise leader
you want to be

Ian J Berry

Published by Customer Centred Consulting Pty Ltd

(trading name Changing What's Normal)

The author welcomes conversation about any aspects of this book.

www.ianberry.biz

email: ian@ianberry.biz

Phone: +61 418 807 898

Copyright © 2020 Ian Berry

Cover design by Jessica Berry pekkaladesign@gmail.com

This book is copyright. Apart from any fair dealing for the purpose of private study, research, criticism, or review, as permitted under the Copyright Act, no part may be reproduced by any process without written permission from the publisher.

All effort was made to render this book free from error and omission. However, the author, publisher, editor, their employees or agents shall not accept responsibility for injury, loss or damage to any person or body or organisation acting or refraining from action as a result of material in this book, whether or not such injury, loss or damage is in any way due to any negligent act or omission, breach of duty, or default on the part of the author, publisher, editor or their employees or agents.

National Library of Australia

Cataloguing-in-Publication data

Berry, Ian

Heart-Leadership: Become the wise leader you want to be

ISBN 978-0-9581236-9-3

Contents

Prologue ... 7

Sparkenation One
Harmony Matters ... 17

Sparkenation Two
Hear Your Heart and The Hearts of Other People
(People Leadership) ... 24

Sparkenation Three
Ask Your Head and Value Greatly The Minds of Others
(Process Innovation) ... 61

Sparkenation Four
Engage Your Hands and Those of Other People
(Progress Sustainability) ... 107

Sparkenation Five
Happenstance -
is a consequence of harmony, heart, head, and hands ... 151

Epilogue ... 156

Acknowledgements ... 167

About Ian ... 173

Prologue

"In the past, jobs were about muscles, now they're about brains, but in future they'll be about the heart."

Minouche Shafik, Director of The London School of Economics, and once a candidate to lead the Bank of England.

Heart-Leadership has three pillars

1. People leadership,
2. Process innovation,
3. Progress sustainability.

I'll define these three shortly.

The three working together create a powerful and unique energy that enables the essentials of a thriving enterprise, namely people feeling valued, living values, and delivering and exchanging value.

Such energy has many faces including Buoyancy, Effervescence, Enthusiasm, Drive, Passion, Pizzazz, Spark, Sparkle, Spirit, Strength, Vibrancy, Vitality, Vigour. Zip.

Heart-Leaders enhance energy, hold it when required, and shift it whenever appropriate.

> *"The secret of change is to focus all of your energy, not on fighting the old, but on building the new."*
>
> **Socrates**

When we lead and respond with our heads we are fighting the old. When we lead and respond with our hearts we are embracing the new and, I believe, possibility.

"Where the attention goes energy flows, and the results show." says my colleague **Nigel Risner**[1].

For just over three years I have been giving my undivided attention to leading with and responding to what happens with my heart first and then my head. I had been in the habit of leading and responding with my head.

My attention shift has been a catalyst to becoming calmer, clearer and more considered. As a consequence I'm more valuable and my impact and contribution are greater.

My discoveries include the following:

Your heart always knows.

Feelings precede thoughts.

Feelings come from your heart.

> *"Most of us think of ourselves as thinking creatures that feel,
> but we are actually feeling creatures that think."*
> ### Dr Jill Bolte Taylor[2]

Feelings are an inner knowing.

Feelings have a different energy, a different frequency or vibration to thoughts.

Thoughts are from our past. Feelings are from our present and future.

The heart knows why and what, the head decides how, and the hands take care of who, where and when.

I have come to understand that this is the natural order of things.

I learned and practised for much of my life that the head ruled and that the brain was in control.

In my life today I use Harmony, Heart, Head, Hands, Happenstance as a mnemonic.

Harmony within ourselves, I have determined, is a precondition to hearing our hearts, asking our heads and then engaging our hands. Happenstance (coincidence, serendipity, synchronicity) follows.

I'll share Sparkenations in this book in the flow of harmony, heart, head, hands and happenstance.

I'll regularly suggest possible actions and close each section with the words *'Do Your Work'*.

A Sparkenation is *a spark that ignites passion that leads to action that changes what's normal.*

What I sense, say and shine a light on in this book is important, yet nowhere near as important as what you hear yourself say to yourself, who you become and how you do your one-of-a-kind work.

'Do Your Work' is inspired by Steven Pressfield's book 'Do The Work'.

'Do The Work' is about overcoming resistance.

Steven believes, and I agree, that the pain of running away from doing what we know we should is greater than actually doing the work.

The very best leaders lead with and from their hearts

I sense a movement gathering momentum fast. Not a movement that is focused on single issues like climate change, police brutality or political corruption. This movement focuses on being fully alive humans and encompasses all the issues where we are failing one another and the environments in which we live.

I sense this just-in-time movement is global. For sure there are local and national solutions. It's just that we are one human race, each of us is different for certain, yet not divided as many in positions of power and influence would have us believe.

There are several world and business leaders who appear to have lost their minds. A new kind of leadership is needed. This kind of leadership is noticeable and inspiring through its coherence.

Heads of State like New Zealand's Jacinda Ardern[3] are showing the way. She is leading with and from her heart. She is demonstrating in a powerful and non-violent way that we can be human and be a politician!

2020 marked thirty years of deep engagement for me in leadership development through being a mentor for leaders as well as giving presentations, conducting workshops and master-classes, and engaging in numerous conversations.

I've been honoured to work with more than 1000 leaders, women and men, in over 40 countries.

Since 2012 I've focused on my own style of presentation/conversations with primarily small groups of people both in person and online.

I've been able to observe and interact with leaders up close and personal and from a myriad of industries. I've been involved in organisations of all shapes and sizes, small, medium and large, family and privately owned, purpose-driven corporations, professional service firms and professional service providers.

I've also been privileged to work with many leaders and their teams over several years.

One thing stands out in all of my work, the very best leaders lead with and from their hearts.

Heart-Leadership is being decisively human in a decidedly digital world

I'm in no doubt that we live in a decidedly digital world because of the dominance of the so-called FAANG organisations (Facebook, Apple, Amazon, Netflix and Google)[4].

Heart-Leadership is a digitally-savvy, human-centred design approach to living. Heart-Leadership has three pillars as previously referenced. Here are their definitions as promised:

1. Hear Your Heart (People Leadership) is the art of seeing, sometimes unearthing, mostly magnifying and enhancing people's essence including your own.

2. Ask Your Head (Process Innovation) is the collaborative work of ensuring processes make it simple for people to bring their essence to their work. (NB processes include policies, procedures, practices, philosophies, principles, structures and systems).

3. Engage Your Hands (Progress Sustainability) is the joyful craft of ensuring progress towards possibility (desired new reality, shared goal/objective/aim) is kept visible.

Paul Schmeja is the CEO of First Contact, world leaders in concierge services and the employee and customer experience.

Paul is a long term Heart-Leadership Enthusiast and a highly valued resident of my Heart-Leadership Online Village. Below is great insight from Paul into People Leadership - when it's thriving and when it's not.

"I was a junior manager in what was regarded then as the best deluxe hotel in Australia, and awarded so for three consecutive years. This boutique hotel on the edge of Melbourne was a home away from home for the rich and famous, the guest list a revolving door of rock bands,

pro tennis players and Hollywood movie stars.

The hotel operated with the tagline "expect the very best", a philosophy led from the top-down with a General Manager who understood the value in taking care of employees as well as guests.

Employee meals were an Award requirement, but this hotel saw an opportunity to do a little better. Staff meals were cooked to order, from a menu prepared weekly by the trainee chefs.

Meal breaks were something to look forward to in a shift... not just filling hungry tummies, but creating an environment for team members to enjoy tasty and wholesome meals while relaxing in the company of colleagues. Also a great opportunity for junior chefs to learn menu planning and practice their trade with their own colleagues as "guests".

A few years into my tenure, the hotel changed hands, The new owners, on a cost-cutting drive, cancelled many employee benefits, starting with replacing staff meals with something that could only be described as "functional".

What message did this send to the employees? That they didn't matter. This was combined with cuts to staffing levels, resources and operating parameters. "Expect the very best.." was eventually even cut from the branding."

My friend and colleague from The Right Company Jacquie Landeman, was a participant in the inaugural Heart-Leadership Online Program. Jacquie captures the Process Innovation pillar profoundly.

She says:

"Tasks driven by policy and procedure have a way of pulling us in to fear and then into resistance.

When I operate from the heart first, I'm reminded that each customer is a "one-of-a-kind-human-being" (thank you Ian!), someone I honour and care for. It helps me to do work I feel good about - where I have shown each person I interact with, respect, kindness and generosity.

I think operating from the heart is why I have finally found meaning, purpose and flow in my work and why I often say to myself "I love my job." And I'm not saving lives, just working in finance."

Donovan Ryan is an IT leader for a government agency. I was honoured to be a mentor for Donovan for over a year. He has also been a regular participant in my monthly Sparkenation conversations, is a resident of my Heart-Leadership Online Village, and was a participant in the inaugural Heart-Leadership Enhancement Program.

When it comes to implementing insights and keeping progress sustainable Donovan is a Star. When something resonates with Donovan he implements with his team and/or his bosses.

"Recently I organised a small cohort from different sections within my organisation, the purpose of this group was for each person to develop the change they were seeking to make with their work. The result from the team after a two week sprint was a new induction process for new starters, a framework for being more resilient, different approaches to communicating with the public, and a new way of thinking about managing organisational change".

The three pillars are bookended by harmony and happenstance.

Harmony is perhaps my favourite all time word.

Hearing my parents and others sing in harmony is a favourite childhood memory. I learned to sing in harmony myself. In my youth I was part of various bands where harmony was a feature of our work.

Singing in harmony is a favourite pastime for my wife Carol and I when we travel in the car. It's a reminder for us of how the world can be.

We humans were meant to live in harmony with each other and our planet. Such harmony must be your intention otherwise Heart-Leadership is not possible.

Happenstance (coincidence/serendipity/synchronicity) is a consequence of the coherence of harmony as an intention, and the harmony of heart, head and hands working together.

The foundations under the pillars.

Leading with heart means being a fully live human being (spiritually alive, emotionally healthy, mentally alert, physically active and universally aware). It's about being decisively human in a decidedly digital world.

Leading with heart means treating people equally, with respect, and taking into account the feelings of people as well as their unique circumstances.

Leading with heart means speaking from your heart, being with all your heart, and following your heart regardless of how other people are being.

I define leadership in general as *the art of inspiring people to see and bring the best out in themselves and other people.*

The first kind of leadership is self-leadership. No one can lead successfully without first leading self.

All change is personal first. Self-leadership is everyone's business. It all begins with self-awareness which I regard as the number one leadership skill.

Self-awareness has much to do with hearing our heart.

Research by the folks at HeartMath[5] has shown that *"the heart is a key component of the emotional system. Scientists now understand that the heart not only responds to emotion, but that the signals generated by its rhythmic activity actually play a major part in determining the quality of our emotional experience from moment to moment."*

As we shall see when we are operating in our one-of-a-kind rhythm and have awareness of the rhythm of others we are Heart-Leaders.

The number two skill of leadership is awareness of others which is the realm of the second kind of leadership that of leading for others.

Leading for others has much to do with fully appreciating people and knowing them in their hearts. One way we do this is through sustaining shared-view in the seven areas of significance that I have explored in previous works - reality, possibility, purpose, strategy, execution, progress and culture.

I will explore shared-view more later. For now to be up to date with the concept and how it can work in your context, please review the short podcasts and videos on each of the seven at http://www.ianberry.biz/sustaining-shared-view/

The third kind of leadership is leading for leaders. This is arguably the toughest kind of leadership.

Leading for leaders is the daily practice of inspiring people to fully appreciate and bring out the best in themselves and other people.

It's all about ensuring other people feel valued, live values and deliver and exchange value, and that they are inspiring others to feel, live and deliver and exchange.

Success in all three forms of leadership requires a harmony with self, hearing your heart, hearing other people's hearts. It requires a meeting of minds and working together with our hands. All these lead to happenstance.

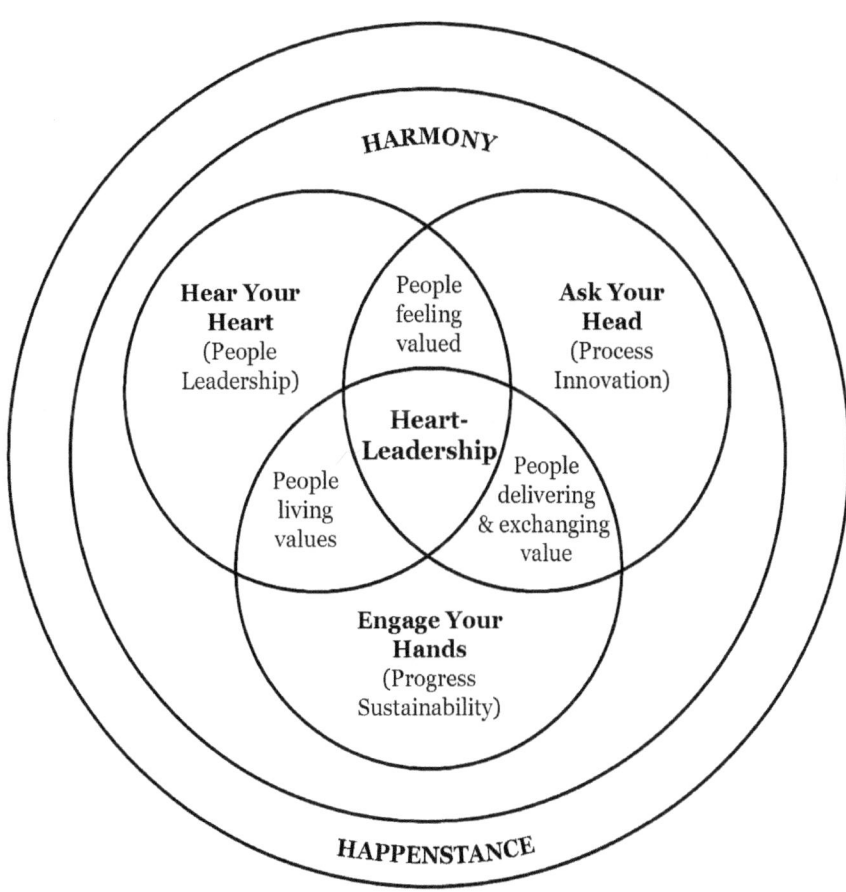

Notes

1   https://www.nigelrisner.com/

2   http://drjilltaylor.com/

3   https://blog.ianberry.biz/2020/10/jacinda-ardern-is-prime-example-of.html

4   I highly recommend the book 'Don't Be Evil The Case Against Big Tech' by Rana Foroohar for great insights into the digital world.

5   From the book 'The HeartMath Solution'. Learn more at https://www.heartmath.com/

Sparkenation One

Harmony Matters

**Heart-Leadership and it's three pillars
is the great harmoniser**

Heart-Leadership puts people first
and leads to people feeling valued,
living values
and delivering and exchanging value.

My first email address when I began self-employment in 1990 was harmonymatters@. It was, in part, a statement of my fundamental belief that the best in life happens when we are in harmony with ourselves, with other people and with our planet.

The idea of harmony is perhaps best illustrated in the ancient Chinese philosophy of yin and yang.

"Yin and yang can be thought of as complementary (rather than opposing) forces that interact to form a dynamic system in which the whole is greater than the assembled parts. According to this philosophy, everything has both yin and yang aspects (for instance, shadow cannot exist without light). Either of the two major aspects may manifest more strongly in a particular object, depending on the criterion of the observation." [1]

My first newsletter for my clients in 1990 was called 'Harmony Matters'. I wrote about overcoming the conflict, difficulty and disagreements in relationships and organisational life and how seeking and sustaining harmony between what sometimes seemed to be opposing forces was a key to happiness and bringing our best to our work.

I observe many apparent opposing forces in the workplace. I make a difference to my clients through working with them to bring these forces together in harmony.

There are:

Relationships and tasks,

Processes and outcomes,

Commitment and competency,

Influence and standards,

People and systems,

Effectiveness and efficiency,

Growth and sustainability,

Bosses and employees,

Masculine and feminine,

Leadership and management,

to name just a few areas where there can be tension that is not helpful and therefore achievements are far less than what is possible.

I agree with the following insight from the great book 'Humanocracy'[2] by Gary Hamel and Michele Zanini

> *"Individuals who resist 'either/or' thinking and deal constructively with paradox are at an advantage. Their responses are nuanced and sophisticated , and represent a better fit with the reality of the world around them."*

The great disharmony is between leadership and management. It's caused by business owners, bosses, executives and shareholders holding onto the concept of people management, an oxymoron if ever there was one.

I will argue strongly here that people cannot be managed and that the concept (in my opinion), like traditional religion, like modern day politics of all persuasions, and profit driven corporations, is actually about controlling the masses for the benefit of a few people.

Traditional management owes it roots to many people. For our purposes here I'll refer to five people, Henry Fayol, Frederick Taylor, Peter Drucker, Mary Parker Follett, and Marvin Bower.

Henry Fayol was a French engineer and mining executive. He and his colleagues are responsible for the planning, organising, staffing, directing, and controlling model still practiced by many today. Fayol lived from 1841 - 1925.

At the same time as Fayolism, as it was often known, Frederick Taylor, also an engineer, was creating what he called 'scientific management'. He became one of the first management consultants of the kind that I personally despise, they have solutions and are out looking for problems. Taylor published The Principles of Scientific Management in 1911.

Taylor's concept was based on the following four principles:

1. "Replace rule-of-thumb work methods with methods based on a scientific study of the tasks.
2. Scientifically select, train, and develop each employee rather than passively leaving them to train themselves.
3. Provide "Detailed instruction and supervision of each worker in the performance of that worker's discrete task" (Montgomery 1997: 250).
4. Divide work nearly equally between managers and workers, so that the managers apply scientific management principles to planning the work and the workers actually perform the tasks."[3]

Of course there's value in the ideas of Fayol and Taylor and other management theorists. Today I apply their insights to process and not to people, hence my concept of process innovation being one of the three pillars of Heart-Leadership, the other two being people leadership and progress sustainability. I believe process innovation is 21st century management.

Heart-Leadership overall is an alternative to people, performance and change management.

It's about leading people and managing processes, all the while ensuring that progress is sustainable.

The so-called father of management Peter Drucker was onto this a long time ago.

Sadly many people forget Drucker's edict - *"One does not manage people—the task is to lead people. And the goal is to make productive the specific strengths and knowledge of each individual.*[4]*"*

Drucker defined leadership as *"The lifting of man's vision to higher sights. The raising of a man's performance to a higher standard. The building of a man's personality beyond its normal limitations."*

Whilst accepting that language in the 1950's was very masculine, the majority of these pioneers of management were oblivious to the feminine energy and therefore encouraged further disharmony.

Mary Parker Follett was an exception. She is one of my Leadership heroes. Largely ignored in her day because she was a women in 1924[5] she wrote:

> *"Leadership is not defined by the exercise of power but by the capacity to increase the sense of power among those led.*
>
> *The most essential work of the leader is to create more leaders."*

Instead of emphasising industrial and mechanical components, or seeing people as replaceable cogs in an organisational machine, as many of her contemporaries advocated, Follett saw what, for her, was the far more important human element.

In many circles we persist in referring to people as resources, as assets, or as capital, the other dreadful yet common expression.

In my mind such labels dehumanise people.

I am all about changing this.

I am re-humanising work with great respect for the many people I know who have HR in their career title. I know their label doesn't signify who they really are or what they do.

Trying to manage people is the great disharmoniser. People cannot be managed.

Performance and change cannot be managed either.

People, performance and change management, along with strategic planning are the great oxymorons of business.

I repeat Heart-Leadership is an alternative to people, performance and change management.

The Strategic Heartistry[6] program that I co-created with Susan Furness is an alternative to strategic planning.

Heart-Leadership and it's three pillars is the great harmoniser. It puts people first and leads to people feeling valued, living values and delivering and exchanging value.

Turning Possibility Into Reality - further suggested actions

- See every person as a leader.

- Make leadership development a priority. Start by reading this excerpt[7] from the book 'The Will To Lead' by Marvin Bower, McKinsey's managing partner from 1950 to 1967. He was ahead of his time advocating the abandoning of command and control structures long before most people.

- Remove, over time, the words 'resources', 'assets', 'capital' where these words refer to people, from all your language, documents and titles.

- Ensure all your design is human-centred.

- Put people first in all the interactions and transactions of your business.

- Look for the harmony point between what seem like opposing forces.

Do Your Work.

Notes

1 https://en.wikipedia.org/wiki/Yin_and_yang

2 https://www.humanocracy.com/

3 https://en.wikipedia.org/wiki/Frederick_Winslow_Taylor

4 'The Practice of Management' (1954)

5 'The Creative Experience' published in 1924

6 https://strategicheartistry.com/

7 https://www.mckinsey.com/featured-insights/leadership/developing-leaders-in-a-business#

Sparkenation Two

Hear Your Heart and The Hearts of Other People (People Leadership)

Your heart knows.

Once you learn to hear and trust your heart's voice you will cease to second guess yourself.

Overview

People leadership is the art of seeing, sometimes unearthing, mostly magnifying and enhancing people's essence including your own.

It's all about hearing your heart and making heart connections with other people.

In this Sparkenation we're exploring:

- Identifying, living and deepening your essence (your one-of-a-kind personal significance).

- Choosing, radiating and honouring and sharing joy.

- Defining your roles at home, work and in third places that best align with your essence and what brings you joy.

Identify your essence
and inspire others to identify theirs

Essence

> *"the intrinsic nature or indispensable quality of something, especially something abstract, which determines its character."*

Find your voice, sing your song, play your music, and help other people to do the same

My favourite metaphors for essence are voice, song and music.

I was first introduced to these metaphors for essence on the day I left hospital following what had been a life-saving operation.

I was 23 years old at the time and, as I look back, I realise I was very naive then about matters of the heart.

My doctor had introduced me to the heart-mind-body connection and had begun to teach me meditation, something which I was totally unfamiliar with.

He gave me a mantra *'I have an attitude of gratitude'* to help ensure that I became a survivor of, what was then, a one in five chance. I became the one using this mantra to tap into my heart. I believed what my doctor was teaching me even though I had very little understanding at the time.

My doctor came to see Carol and I on the day I could finally go home after weeks in hospital. His parting words were *"Don't die with your music locked in you."*

Carol and I had no idea what he meant! We later learned that music was a metaphor for essence.

Later still we discovered that the expression *don't die with your music locked in you* was by the British Prime Minister Benjamin Disraeli who probably borrowed the words from Samuel Beckett.

I began to take my essence seriously. I became passionate about my essence and the essence of other people.

I gradually began to notice more the nuance in people. I became curious and committed to understanding myself and other people as

26 Heart Leadership

fully as possible.

These discoveries were the beginning of a what has become my life's work to inspire people to find your voice, sing your song, play your music and for you to inspire others to do the same.

The Stephen R. Covey book that I recommend the most, 'The 8th Habit From Effectiveness to Greatness', digs deep into this topic.

In this book Covey describes Voice as *"unique personal significance - significance that is revealed as we face our greatest challenges and which makes us equal to them."*

He says Voice is found at the nexus of talent, need, conscience and passion as illustrated below:

According to Covey

Talent *(your natural gifts and strengths),*

Need *(including what the world needs enough to pay you for),*

Conscience *(that still small voice within that assures you of what is right and that prompts us to actually do it),*

Passion *(those things that naturally energise, excite, motivate and inspire you).*

What are your natural gifts and strengths?

What needs are you providing that you're being paid for?

What is that small still voice inside you saying to you on a consistent basis?

What naturally energises, excites, motivates and inspires you?

These four questions demand answers don't they?

The world needs you to have found your Voice!

Sometimes we call your Voice Song and sometimes Music.

In many of my online conversations and in-person forums I ask participants to choose a theme song for where their life is heading. Many people immediately get their smart phone out and play their song!

What would your theme song be right now?

My theme song currently is 'This is the moment'[1]

This is the moment; this is the day
When I send all my doubts and demons on their way.
Every endeavor I have made ever
Is coming into play, is here and now today.

This is the moment, this is the time
When the momentum and the moment are in rhyme
Give me this moment, this momentous moment;
I'll gather up my past, and make some sense at last.

This is the moment, when all I've done
All of the dreaming, scheming and screaming become one.
This is the day, just see it shine
When all I've lived for becomes mine.

This is the moment, this is the hour
When I can open tomorrow like a flower.
And with my hand to, everything I've planned to
Fulfill my grand design; see all my stars align;

This is the moment, my final test;
Destiny beckoned, I never reckoned second best.
I won't look down, I must not fall;
This is the moment, the sweetest moment of them all.

This is the moment, forget all the odds
This day or never I'll sit forever with the gods.
When I look back I will recall, moment for moment
This was the moment,
The greatest moment of them all.

Every word of 'This is the moment' can grab me in a myriad of ways at any given time.

Whenever I play the song (my favourite is the Anthony Warlow version), the words inspire me to hear my heart and ignore my head temporarily.

Self-doubt happens in our heads.

Over time we have taught ourselves stories we replay whenever we feel as if we are under threat or however the feeling of inadequacy is manifesting itself.

When we get into the habit of hearing our heart before we give our heads any audience, we begin to recognise our one-of-a-kind Voice, our essence.

Your heart knows.

Once you learn to hear and trust Your essence you will cease to second guess yourself.

Live your essence

"To be who we are,

and to become all that we are capable of becoming,

is the only purpose in life."

Robert Louis Stevenson

Over my 30 years as a mentor for leaders with heart I have observed and gotten to know many great leaders.

Below are the gifts (another word for essence) that I observe the most.

As you read through the list listen to your heart.

Which gifts resonate with you?

Which ones would you regard as integral to who you are?

Which gifts will you choose to enhance?

Being

Presence: gift for attracting good just by being true to oneself,

Spiritual: gift for understanding the interconnectedness of all things,

Integrity: gift for saying what we mean and meaning what we say,

Trust: gift for being trustworthy.

Intention

Service: gift for giving without expectation of getting back,

Purpose: gift for being clear of purpose in life and living it,

Ethics: gift for doing things right and doing the right thing,

Driven: gift for not being sidetracked no matter what the hurdles may be.

Feeling

Empathy: gift for feeling with others,

Interpersonal: gift for getting on with people,

Enthusiasm: gift for being inspirational in any situation,

Understanding: gift for understanding others without judgement or prejudice.

Thinking

Questioning: gift for asking the right questions at the right time,

Visualization: gift for seeing and creating actions in the mind,

Strategic thinking: gift for seeing all the scenarios for the future and choosing the most appropriate direction,

Problem Solving: a gift to think things through and come up with the most appropriate solution.

Doing

Courage: gift for making a stand when no one else is,

Focus: gift for establishing a practice and following it no matter what[2],

Persistence: gift for staying the course and not giving up,

Efficiency: gift for achieving tasks in the best way possible.

In what ways will you enhance your gifts?

I embrace three proven pathways to enhance my gifts:

1. Engage mentors and/or performance possibility partners who help me to identify enhancements and then encourage and support me as I make them.
2. Belong to peer groups where the focus is on personal development as much as professional development.
3. Undertake courses and programs.

What pathways would you add to the above?

Deepen your essence

Deepening our essence requires the deliberate daily practice of invoking the qualities of the heart.

There are a number of diagnostic tools that can help us to understand and deepen our essence.

The first I recommend is 'The Vitality Test'[3].

This test is based in Chinese philosophy. Its creator Nick Haines worked in Chinese medicine for thirty-five years. Nick and his business partner Matthew Newnham were mentors for me in 2015. I found their insights into my essence remarkable and highly valuable.

'The Vitality Test' has five energy descriptors:

The Reflector *(water energy).*

The Innovator *(wood energy).*

The Connector *(fire energy).*

The Assimilator *(earth energy),.*

and ***The Completer*** *(metal energy).*

The test was incredibly accurate in describing my wood energy strengths as well as the pitfalls. Many of my clients have also benefited from undertaking 'The Vitality Test'.

The second diagnostic I recommend is 'The Edgewalkers Profile Assessment'[4].

The Edgewalker qualities and skills resonate with me.

I'm sure you will also find that undertaking their profile assessment is worthwhile. You'll receive a good report. I personally find the development suggestions in the report valuable.

The Edgewalker Qualities

Self-Awareness

Awareness of your thoughts, values, and behavior and a commitment to spend time in self-reflection with the goal of becoming a better person.

Passion

An intense focus on your purpose or the use of your gifts in a way that adds value to your life and the world.

Integrity

A commitment to live in alignment with your core values, to align your words and your behavior, to keep your word.

Vision

The gift of being able to see what others cannot – possibilities, trends, the future, guidance from the spiritual.

Playfulness

A joyful sense of fun and creativity, and an ability to keep everything in perspective.

The Edgewalker Skills

Sensing the Future

The ability to understand and know the future.

Risk-Taking

The ability to try what hasn't been tried before, to trust your instincts, and to break new ground.

Manifesting

The ability to take a thought, idea, or vision and take practical steps to bring it into being.

Focusing

The ability to be very centered and to give all your attention to an action or project that has significance and importance

Connecting

The ability to see and build unique connections between people, tasks, and ideas.

Magnifying and enhancing is a great way to deepen your essence

Self-leadership, leading for others and leading for leaders all thrive when magnifying and enhancing your essence, and the essence of other people is a priority.

Find out what makes people feel valued and provide it.

I have asked many people over the past decade during forums and master-classes to complete the following sentence,

I feel valued when …?

How would you complete the sentence?

The most common responses are

… I'm being acknowledged for my contribution.

… others take the time to appreciate me or my work.

… I feel listened to.

Invoking the qualities of the heart

In the wonderful book 'The Heart Math Solution'[5] the authors reference often what they call core heart qualities. My favourites are love, gratitude, appreciation, care, happiness, compassion, harmony and kindness.

Deepening our essence requires the deliberate daily practice of invoking the qualities of the heart.

Here's some heart reflections of mine on these qualities:

Love

The Ancient Greeks had four words for love. Two are well known - eros (romantic love) and agape (love in a spiritual sense).

The other two are not generally as well known. There's storge, meaning natural affection like parents feel for their children.

And then there's philia. This is the one I find the most insightful for Heart-Leaders. Philia is often translated as affectionate regard or friendship. We need more philia in our organisations. It will lead to more philia in the world. And we need it right?

I find it simple (but not always easy) to have affectionate regard for people because I know everyone of us is a one-of-a-kind human being. Only the hardest of hearts cannot love a one-off.

Philia love is a foundation stone of Heart-Leadership.

Gratitude

Carol and I walk with our dog Molly every day, rain, hail or shine.

A ritual we have adopted is to express out loud what we're grateful for. It really sets up the remainder of the day for us.

We're well practiced in gratitude. We know that being truly grateful for what we have leads to more of what we need.

Being grateful is something I have practiced daily now for forty-three years. I was 23 years old when I faced a life-threatening operation with a one in five survival rate.

I became the one largely because my surgeon taught me gratitude. In preparing for the operation that saved my life I followed his instructions to stand in front of the mirror and say out loud *"I have an attitude of gratitude."* I have been carrying out this ritual every day since!

In the best and worst of times I have learned that being grateful and having *"an attitude of gratitude"* is the key to living a happy and contented life.

Having *"an attitude of gratitude"* is a foundation stone of Heart-Leadership.

Appreciation

I have been researching what employees really want from employers and fellow employees for more than two decades. Appreciation tops the list.

The eminent psychologist William James observed: *"The deepest craving of human nature is the need to be appreciated."*

Feeling appreciated and being willing and able to show appreciation to others are foundation stones of Heart-Leadership.

Care

"People don't care how much you know until they know how much you care." said Theodore Roosevelt, the youngest person to ever be President of the United States and generally regarded in the top five Presidents, not least for his work in ensuring fairness for all people.[6]

Care begins with self-care. As a boy my father taught me that the keys to living a good life were to be spiritually alive, mentally alert and physically active. Over time I added emotionally healthy and universally aware. I called these the five faces of a human being fully alive. Heart-Leaders are fully alive.

Caring for others is to support them in being fully alive human beings. In many of the best workplaces today and also in some countries well-being is measured and seen as more valuable than the traditional economic measures of success.

Caring for self and other people are foundation stones of Heart-Leadership.

Happiness

The Rabbi Hyman Judah Schachtel in an excellent book 'The Real Enjoyment of Living' said:

"Happiness is not having what you want, but wanting what you have."

I contemplate this often.

Such happiness is a foundation stone of Heart-Leadership.

Compassion

There's a lot of truth for me in the following attributed to Fred Kofman, a leader in the conscious business movement:

"Wisdom without compassion is ruthlessness,

and compassion without wisdom is folly."

One of the Apostles of the Christian Church is reported to have said, *"Faith without works is dead."*

A lot of faiths are dead, dying, or in trouble today because the actions of a few of the faithful betray their stated beliefs.

I meet a lot of people who are more interested in being right than in being compassionate for example. Compassion for me is at the truthful heart of all the world's religions. Compassion is not a belief, it's a behaviour.

If we are not living and breathing a compassionate life we render whatever we believe as null and void, regardless of what we say.

A new world is being born. Compassion is a key component. There is a place for faith in this new world. For me belief is personal and therefore deserving of respect.

What really matters in this new world though is behaviour.

Some people have asked me "What has compassion got to do with the future success of my business?" My answer is - Everything! particularly in a world where the leading edge is being purpose driven and people focused. The leading edge is also seeing technology as an enabler and enhancer of the human experience.

Being compassionate is a foundation stone of Heart-Leadership.

Harmony

Harmony matters, perhaps above all else. Living a life at the intersection of yin and yang is the daily quest of the Heart-Leader.

Living in harmony with self, other people and our planet is a foundation stone of Heart-Leadership.

Kindness

There's a one minute and forty-seven seconds video at this blog post https://blog.ianberry.biz/2013/10/differencemaking-is-often-just-moment.html

Please take time to watch it. I have never seen, before or since, a better demonstration of kindness.

Such kindness is a foundation stone of Heart-Leadership.

Which of these heart qualities make your heart sing?

Such resonance is key to your essence?

How can you become more of who you are capable of becoming?

What will you do next?

Maybe begin by sending stars never black holes

In the early 1990's I taught Peter Marshman's Communication Magic program to hundreds of people. A key to the success of the program was teaching people to send stars never back holes in both sending and receiving messages.

Typically stars are messages that promote high self esteem of receivers and the likelihood of personal best performance.

Examples are enthusiastic greetings, smiles, recognition of effort and achievements, compliments, being included, putting ourselves out for others, asking someone else for advice, showing genuine interest

Typically black holes are messages that mean a likely drop in self esteem and the corresponding drop in personal performance.

Examples are not saying hello or greeting people as though they barely exist, not saying thank you or not recognising other people's efforts, claiming the credit for someone else's work, ignoring or excluding people, putting people down, criticism as opposed to constructive critique or feedforward, thinking our way is the only way and demonstrating this in our behaviour, having a closed mind

People must be empowered to deal with black holing or other inappropriate behaviour by responding to poor sending with the statement "I think that's a black hole".

Conversely it is strongly encouraged that star behaviour be complemented with words such as "thanks for the star" or "Thank You. You are a Star."

I had goose bumps when I read the following Star Story on LinkedIn by my friend and colleague and former client Peter Merrett:

LEADING WITH HEART: *A delicious antidote for the moment of now.*

Pick a card, any card

If indeed there was a card, that could symbolise a refreshing antidote to everything we are experiencing this year, which card would you hope it to be? There is no doubt that Clubs, Spades and Diamonds have little use to us at the moment. But Hearts would be warmly welcome and especially useful.

Before I reveal my little example here of a most wondrous heart, any card from the suite of Hearts would work; Ace, Queen, Jack included. Even the Joker would be welcome to add a dash of fun!

But here in this moment, I decided the most fitting card to serve you is The King of Hearts.

It's a card that signifies 'personal qualities of honesty. It represents a kind-hearted and fair man. His gentle temperament makes him a fine friend'.

Here I will magically transform this card into the symbol of a refreshing pick-me-up, for the moment of now.

The habit of heart

We are creatures of habit, even during times as confusing and

unsettling that have faced us this year. But imagine creating a habit that is so small and seemingly insignificant, that you unwittingly change someone's entire day - or even better, challenge their entire way of thinking?

It's a wonderful thought isn't it?

My family's day starts much the same every morning - with school drop-off. An often nerve-testing moment trying to get my two young boys ready to actually leave the house. But it's made that much more enjoyable by the actions of someone at school and the daily habit that they've created for themselves.

Every morning as I arrive at school with the boys, there's a positive buzz that lingers in the air. A buzz of heart and wonder that comes from one person... The school Principal.

It's easy to presume that a school Principal would be the one person you would rarely see in the morning - obviously hidden away in their office surrounded by paperwork, emails, and sorting their busy schedule for the day. But that's certainly not the case here. Believe it or not, my kids actually love arriving at the school gates.

Who would have thought?!

Leadership with heart

As each car crawls slowly along the side road through the carline each morning, there is a constant refreshing vibe that swirls through the morning air. It's his heartful presence.

But it's where he's standing AND what he's doing that makes all the difference. He's not on the playground or at the school gates. He stands outside the school gates, on the other side of the road and does a friendly little wave to each and every car. Over and over again as the parents one-by-one drop their children at the school gates. Greeting all the children with a merry "good morning" as they jump out of the car - smiling as he quickly walks them the few seconds up to the school gates.

His positivity ripples across the whole school

Now, this wasn't a 'nice one-off little gesture' he started when our school was fortunate to reopen a few months ago. No, this is real and *lasting. It's 100% authentic. But he doesn't have to do it, there is no obligation - the sun will still rise and set each day as normal. And yet, there he is - each and every day, rain or shine! He's made it his daily habit. His heart takes him there, and everyone loves it. His positivity ripples across the whole school. Without question, he is the King of Hearts.*

Read Peter's full article[7].

The best story about this is that when I called Peter to get his permission to share his story in this book he told me about how he took a gift wrapped printed version of his LinkedIn article including all the comments and gave it to this Principal. No words exchanged just a deeply shared heart moment.

Turning Possibility Into Reality - further suggested actions

- Undertake my short online course to discover your essence. Its called 'Magnificence' You'll find it at http://www.ianberry.biz/magnificence-online-course/ This course is based around 3 short videos including one where I share my 'Don't die with your music locked in you' story.

- Seek out people you trust and who know you well and ask them to describe, in a sentence or two, your essence when they see you at your very best. I undertook this exercise many years ago and and have stayed with what I was told as follows: "Ian has a special sense of what is and what can be and articulates these in inspiring ways. He then shines a light on possible pathways to take to move to what's next." Sense, say, shine became my personal essence mantra.

- Reflect on your life's work to date. What is it that you love to do more than anything else? What does this tell you about your essence?

- Play with Covey's insights about your talent, need, conscience and passion. Piece everything together and describe your essence in a sentence or two.

- Get used to hearing your heart before you start asking your head anything.

- Commit to inspiring, encouraging and supporting others in seeing, sometimes unearthing, mostly magnifying and enhancing their essence.

Do Your Work.

Choose joy

Recognising what brings us joy in the every day matters of life is a key to ensuring that every day matters.

Joy is a heart disposition. It's a choice we make.

The song below was written by my friend and colleague Glenn Capelli with his mate Keith McDonald. It's based on Brian Keenan's 'An Evil Cradling' book about him being held hostage in Beirut.

"They can damage you but deep inside find a place that they cannot reach and 'choose joy'".

CHOOSE JOY
Let your spirit flow
Let your fingers go
Let your feet start tapping
Let your whole being happen
Let your spirit flow
Let your heart beat know
Every girl and boy
Choose joy choose joy
Choose joy for the morning
Choose joy for the day
Choose joy for the night-time
Choose joy all the way
Let your knee caps bend
Let your bruises mend
Let your burdens drop
Let your belly flop
Let your spirit flow
Let your dance team know
Every girl and boy
Choose joy choose joy
Choose joy for the morning
Choose joy for the day
Choose joy for the night-time
Choose joy all the way
Let your nostrils flex
Let your self impress

Let your freedom fly
Let your heart know why
Oh your spirit flows
And our whole world knows
Every girl and boy
Choose joy choose joy
Choose joy for the springtime
Choose joy for the fall
Choose joy for the sun and the raindrops
Choose joy for it all.

© CAPELLI

Viktor Frankl chose joy in the most difficult of circumstances.

He wrote the following while a prisoner in Auschwitz where over one million people died.[8]

"Between stimulus and response there is a space. In that space is our power to choose our response. In our response lies our growth and our freedom."

Creating harmony between our Heart, Head and Hands is a practical way to act on these insights.

There's a natural order. Heart is first, head second, hands third.

The head tries to dominate and be first. Don't let it. This too is a choice.

My colleague in The Right Company, Anne Roche[9], said the following to another colleague in a forum *"Sometimes the noise in our head drowns out the knowledge in our hearts - I'm glad I could help you turn that noise down so you could hear yourself clearly."*

We can all help others to hear our hearts clearly.

Our quest is to use our heads to work out how to enact the why and what in our hearts and to then trust our hands with the who, when and where.

A mantra I use to choose a response to stimuli rather than react to what happens is 'Start With The Heart'.

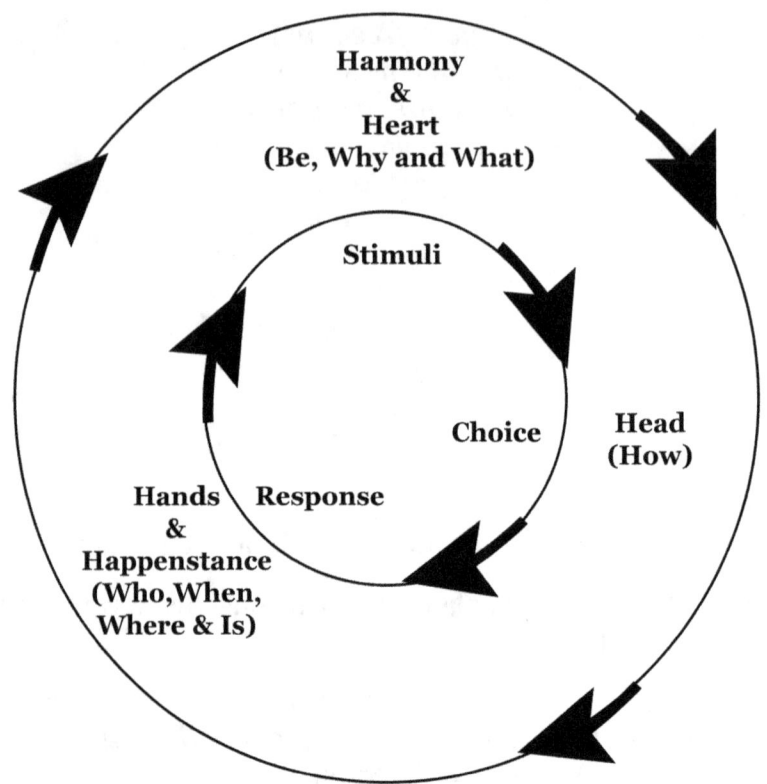

The more I put this mantra into practice the more joyful my life and the less I concern myself with what other people do or don't do.

There's also a wonderful technique I use called FREEZE-FRAME from the folk at HeartMath. I use it regularly to help me to choose joy and to find the most effective ways to live my life.

"The Five Steps of FREEZE-FRAME[10]

1. *Recognise the stressful feeling and FREEZE-FRAME it. Take a time out.*

2. *Make a sincere effort to shift focus away from the racing mind or disturbed emotion to the area of your heart. Pretend you're breathing through your heart to help focus your energy in this area. Keep your focus there for ten seconds or more.*

3. *Recall a positive, fun feeling or time you've had in life and try to re-experience it.*

4. *Now, using your intuition, common sense, and sincerity, ask your heart, What would be a more efficient response to the situation, one that would minimise future stress?*

5. *Listen to what your heart says in answer to your question. (It's an effective way to put your reactive mind and emotions in check and an in-house source of common sense solutions!)"*

Radiate joy even when your work is hard

I do know the value of hard work. My real learning though has come through ensuring that the work is joyful even when it's hard.

Several years ago Carol and I completed the restoration of a one hundred year old property that took us several years part time. We cried as our friends and family shared the joy of the finished product. It was amazing to see the old house with a fresh coat of paint they said.

What was unmentioned was the untold hours of back breaking work and the preparation to get ready to put on the finishing touches of a coat of paint on that made our home look so cared for.

All great work is like this.

Often we feel joy at the end of something rather than recognising our joy throughout as well as on completion.

Carol and I, even when exhausted, were in the habit of stepping back and admiring our progress even when such still looked like a mess. We grew accustomed to finding joy even when the work is hard.

I meet many sales people not making enough sales. I know why their sales are down. Not enough preparation in the hard work of building relationships and giving value in advance and therefore an insufficient number of appointments. There is joy in the process of all these, we just need to acknowledge it.

I meet many people with great ideas that are unexecuted. I know why. It takes a lot of energy to turn information into insight into inspiration that can turn an idea into innovation. There is joy in the process of all these, we just need to acknowledge each piece of the puzzle.

I meet lots of business owners who are not grasping the great opportunities that crises or downturns present. I know why.

These folk are either doing what they have always done and therefore are being out done by those working harder and particularly wiser, or they are focusing on the pain rather than the pleasure of re-imagining and re-starting post the crisis or disruption.

We have a crest adorning a wall in our home The Latin words underneath translate *"Nothing without labour"*.

We believe this was the creed of our family from a very, very long time ago. It isn't marketing people who invented tag lines!

Whether it is our families credo or not I certainly learned the value of hard work from an early age.

Barely a teenager, with my brother four years younger, we built our family home (all except the bricks and tiles on the roof) with our parents and with our bare hands. I remember once my football coach saying to my Father *"Your boy has a great work ethic."* My father, surprised at the remark, simply replied *"He knows the value of hard work."*

I do know the value of hard work. My real learning though has come through ensuring that the work is joyful even when it's hard.

Having a great work ethic is important to being a person of value and in delivering and exchanging value. What is key however is finding joy in the work.

One of the most profound statements I have ever heard comes from the great book 'The Radical Leap' by Steven Farber[11]. It's a wonderful fable with a great message. Steven says *"Do what you love in the service of people who love what you do"*

What an insight.

Are you doing what you love in the service of people who love what you do?

I woke up this morning, as I do every morning, ready to work hard. I know that nothing of value is created or delivered without labour.

Above all though today, like every day, I'm seeking to do what I love in the service of people who love what I do, and to find personal joy in such work.

Honour and share joy

There's perhaps no greater honour in life than to share joy with the people we love.

The more I look for joy in life the more I find it.

I see children riding their bikes without a care in the world.

I see lovers holding hands while walking in the park oblivious to others.

I see joy as I observe an old man sitting on the bench reading what is obviously a favourite book.

Joy is everywhere when we're open to seeing it.

Honouring and sharing joy is being these kind of moments ourselves and with the people we love.

My friend and colleague Bernadette Jiwa's 'A Compass for the Heart'[12] is a lovely way to be prepared to honour and share joy.

Bernadette's book is a ninety day journal that I began myself while writing this book. I highly recommend it.

I vividly remember the moment Carol received her first engagement as a marriage celebrant.

It came by surprise by text from an old friend saying *"Damian and I have decided to get married and we would love you to marry us."*

Carol's journey to this point had been very challenging. We re-lived the hard moments of her journey for a few minutes and then basked in the glory of joy that this new moment had brought her.

What are your honouring and sharing joy stories?

Turning Possibility Into Reality - further suggested actions

- Over the next week or so write down a joy story for every 5 years of your life. Note the feelings this exercise bring you in your heart.

- Recall the moments in your life where you have worked really hard. Do you most remember the results or the journey to them? Make a decision to celebrate joy several times every day.

- Make a list of the songs that have brought you and your loved ones, your friends and colleagues joy. Play them again with these people. Make a favourite list in Spotify or whatever app you use.

- Become an ambassador of joy whatever this may mean for you.

- Practice hearing your heart first and instructing your head to be quiet until you ask for help. Make this a habit.

Do Your Work.

Relationships and roles at home, at work and in third places

In Heart-Leadership everyone has places to be, roles to fulfill, and communities to contribute to.

"Home is the place where, when you have to go there, they have to take you in." said the poet Robert Frost.

First place home, second place work, third place everywhere else. All have changed DC (during coronavirus) haven't they?

I sense more changes AC (after coronavirus) as well as taking the good from DC (during coronavirus) into the future.

First place home

Many people are telling me that they have a renewed enthusiasm for family and a greater appreciation of family members as a positive consequence of coronavirus.

I feel that this will continue and contribute to a more peaceful world. What do you feel?

I also hear of increases in personal stress, domestic violence and suicide as negative consequences of coronavirus.

What do you hear your heart suggesting to you in terms of how you could help other people?

Second place work

Will the workplace ever be as it was BC (before coronavirus)?

I hope not.

In my book The Appreciative Leader I overviewed what I see as the new world of work. On the next page is a table of this.

Old World of Work	New world of Work
Bureaucracy	Decisive actions in moments of truth
Blame/Shame/Spin	Accountability/Appreciation/Authenticity
Competition	Collaboration
Compromise	Co-promise
Corruption	Co-operatives/networks
Cultures of control	Cultures of Candour
Delivering returns to shareholders	Delivering value to all stakeholders
Dictatorship/ my way is the only way	Difference/finding a way together
Favouring the few	Enabling everyone to enhance their gifts
Focus in economics	Focus on solving society's problems
Fixed ways of doing things	Flexibility/Adaptability
Goal-based	Value-based
Greed	Gratitude
Institutions/boys clubs	Individuals/Equity of opportunity
Interrupting the masses	Engaging in niches/tribes/communities
Jobs/job security/jobs for life	Roles/Alliances/Network Intelligence/Alumni
Managing people	Leading people/managing processes
Machines	Gardens
Men	Men and Women
Partisan	Bi-partisan
Performance appraisals/formality	Candid/convivial conversations/informality
Planet exploitation/destruction	Planet protection/regeneration
Politics	People
Results	Reasons and Relationships
Self-interest	Enlightened self-interest
Sticking with the status quo	Changing What's Normal
Strategic planning/change management	Strategy in a sentence/Change Leadership
Unsolicited feedback	Requested 'feedforward' and feedback
Venture capitalism	Crowd-sourcing/crowd-funding
'Wall Street' 'Phantom wealth'	'Main Street' 'Real Wealth'

It's four years since I made these observations. It warms my heart to see that many people are making the shift from old to new!

Many people have expressed to me the desire to continue to work from home. Of course this is possible for many of us.

I note that highly successful organisations such at Atlassian[13], Twitter and Facebook are now making working from home normal.

My sense is that less traffic by car, less plane travel, and less urban life would be good for people as well as the planet. Do you agree?

Third place everywhere else

BC (before coronavirus) I met with my clients online and in person. Most of the in-person meetings were in coffee shops, restaurants or a hotel lobby because people often wanted to get away from the office! I expect that AC (after coronavirus) this will continue. Who knows, maybe the office will become a third place where we meet up just to connect as human beings.

Of course online Zoom has become the third place.

I was already comfortable in the Zoom room. Now there's more rooms because Zoom have added a great breakout facility!

I have very much enjoyed my experiences using this addition to their offering.

I'm continuing to make my conversations online as human-centred as possible. One way I do this is by not having voice-over slides.

You'll find the video of the latest such conversation at https://www.ianberry.biz/online-and-in-person-events/

My sense is more Zooming even AC (after-coronavirus). What are you sensing? My deeper sense-making is that we will cherish both our in-person and online third places more than we ever have.

There is turmoil in many parts of the wider world at the moment. I believe this is largely about the self-centred and the self-righteous ones trying to hang onto a world that benefited them and not everyone else. I want to see this world end.

I cannot do anything about it directly though. What I can do is be better and wiser and more valuable in the world's that I co-exist in, both online and in person. What can you do?

When we all do this the wider world will benefit.

I wish you well in your world and the first, second and third places where you belong.

People don't have jobs. We have roles

Dispense with job descriptions and watch your people soar.

One of the most deeply demotivating documents in the workplace is the job description!

The problem I see with most job descriptions is that they list tasks and say very little about relationships or value delivery, the two matters about which every role in your business must be about.

Most often, down at the bottom of the form are the words *"and anything else as directed."* As I say, highly demotivating.

Job descriptions are a hangover from the Industrial Revolution and they still cause headaches.

Role clarity statements, my recommended replacement for job descriptions, improve well-being.

Dispense with job descriptions and watch your people soar.

Every person in your workplace has a role: to deliver value to and to exchange value with other people. Value that we all demand, desire, and feel that we deserve. I sometimes refer to these as must have's, should have's and nice-to-haves.

"Your customer is whoever gets your work next." said the great Japanese management thinker Kaoru Ishikawa.

I highly recommend taking Iskikawa's concept to heart and undertake a value delivery and exchange review and then, in collaboration, upgrade everyone's role clarity statements.

Here's a template I use with my clients:

I call it Value Exchange and Delivery Refresh.

	Relationships	Task and Transactions	The Experience
Must Receive			
Should Receive			
Nice to Receive			

Giver: Receiver:
Date:

Upgrading to role clarity statements.

With your people, document who their customers are (relationships) and what value must be delivered to and/or exchanged with each person.

I've helped hundreds of my clients to dispense with job descriptions and replace them with role clarity statements. Below are the headings we use.

In conjunction with Performance Possibility Plans or plans-on-a-page (we will explore these in the next section), role clarity statements enable conversations about performance to be elevated and lead to greater responsibility.

Do this work and, in the space of a few weeks, you can expect greater value being delivered, and exchanged, by everyone. This will mean happier employees and happier external customers.

What would you and your employees write under these headings?

1. Workplace or Business Purpose
2. Role Purpose
3. Key Accountabilities and Responsibilities
4. Key Performance Measures and Key Human Indicators (Lead

measures)

5. Key Relationships of the role and the value that must be delivered to each person
6. Key outcomes of role (Lag measures)
7. Required levels of commitment (will) and competency (skill)
8. Key gifts/talents (essence) required and that need to be enhanced to excel in role and prepare for future roles
9. Learning and development and career path opportunities

All of the above can be outlined on two sides of an A4 page at the most.

There are some examples of the use of this template at https://www.ianberry.biz/wp-content/uploads/2015/08/Roleclarityexample.pdf

People don't have jobs. We have relationships with other people where value delivery and exchange is paramount to the enjoyment of the relationships and the success of the organisation.

Hawthorn Football Club case study and Bill's story

In 2015 the Hawthorn Football Club won their third successive Australian Football League (AFL) premiership. This feat has only been achieved six times in the history of the AFL.

I'm not a supporter of the club. I do admire them greatly.

Their Play Your Role campaign is one action you can emulate and immediately improve your business. Learn more at https://www.hawthornfc.com.au/news/393009/play-your-role

Bill's story

For over a quarter of a century I've been helping my clients to dispense with job descriptions and replace them with role clarity statements. It all began when I met Bill.

I first met Bill in the early nineties. I was in the early days of doing discovery work into how I could best help the organisation where Bill worked. This meant meeting with lots of people in the offices and factory.

I began to notice that each time I came out of a meeting, Bill was close by, leaning on his broom.

Soon curiosity got the better of me so I made a beeline for Bill.

After explaining who I was and what I was doing I asked Bill *"So what's your role?"* *"I thought you'd never ask me."* he replied and then said *"I'm the Assistant to the Managing Director."*

Bill's job was Head Cleaner. His role was of far greater significance than what would normally be felt about such a role.

I invested several hours with Bill and learned everything I needed to know about the organisation.

Included in what I learned from Bill were two insights which he had previously passed onto the management team and that they had failed to act on. When they did take action the bottom-line improved by four million dollars!

What have your employees been sharing with you lately that you haven't yet acted on?

Like the Hawthorn Football Club, every person working in your business has a key role. Not just the star players, every human being. If you're focused on a few and not the many you're missing a magic opportunity in your business.

When everyone is playing their role we all win.

One simple yet profound action. Lead with your heart. Learn about relationships.

Begin today to have conversations with your employees about their roles.

Over time get rid of job descriptions and replace them with role clarity statements.

This is Heart-Leadership work!

Communities are much more valuable than networks

"The greatest gift you can give a person is to see who they are and to reflect that back to them."

Bernadette Jiwa

If you want to understand the difference between a network and a community, ask your Facebook friends to help paint your house says Henry Mintzberg in a piece for Drucker Forum[14].

In an interview Ben Elton[15] says *"The "age of outrage" can largely be blamed on the speed of social progress.*

Communities now are people like you with the same agenda, sexuality, race, creed, religion or politics.

It's not a physical community at all and I think that's a very interesting and confusing time for us all."

I have a positive view about online communities providing they have shared-view about values behaviours and a shared focus.

I have had a private Facebook community group for example. I find it interesting that Facebook is placing more emphasis on groups.

What I particularly love from the work of Henry Mintzberg is the concept of Communityship.[16]

Henry's insights add great value to my long term investment of time, energy and money in communities both in person and online.

In my case there have been many evolutions in the names Differencemakers, Changing What's Normal, Talent Enhancers, Appreciative Leaders, and Maverick Thinkers Farm.

The names have reflected where myself and my clients were focused at a given time. The common thread has been about being the best human beings that we can be.

I currently belong to an international online community The Right Company[17]. One of the founders is best-selling author Bernadette Jiwa. She says:

"The greatest gift you can give a person is to see who they are and to reflect that back to them."

This happens in The Right Company and is a key reason why I belong and contribute.

During the writing of this book I felt in my heart the need and desire to again lead a community.

I let the feeling percolate for a month before forming an overview and then asking eight of my clients for their input. When seven of the eight agreed to be involved I knew in my heart that I was on the right path!

I decided to call this new community The Heart-Leadership Online Village[18] rather than community because of a feeling that the word 'community' has become a bit of a buzz word.

Despite this feeling, at heart, my belief is that communities are a key to our best future. Whatever they may be called, communities are much more valuable than networks.

In a wonderful book 'Sand talk'[19] author Tyson Yunkaporta says " ... *the most destructive idea in existence: I am greater than you; you are less than me.*" True communities help us to extinguish this idea.

Turning Possibility Into Reality - further suggested actions

- Take time out to reflect on the third places you've engaged in and make a note of why you were involved and what you found to be of value.

- Note what you contributed to in these third places you reflected on and how your work made you feel.

- Start to lead your own community online, in person, or both.

- Wherever you belong renew your commitment to making a difference there.

- Determine/create a ritual of your response whenever you feel you are greater than someone else or feel that others are less than you.

- Regularly choose a new world of work theme to work on as a project with your work colleagues or community of people.

Do Your Work.

Notes

1 Songwriters: Frank Wildhorn / Leslie Bricusse

This Is the Moment lyrics © BMG Rights Management, Reservoir Media Management Inc, Shapiro Bernstein & Co. Inc.

2 https://Seths.blog/thepractice/

3 https://www.fiveinstitute.com/the-vitality-test/

4 https://edgewalkers.org/65-2/ and https://edgewalkers.org/edgewalkers/skills/

5 https://www.heartmath.com/

6 https://en.wikipedia.org/wiki/Theodore_Roosevelt

7 https://www.linkedin.com/pulse/leading-heart-peter-merrett/

8 https://en.wikipedia.org/wiki/Viktor_Frankl

9 https://annerochecoaching.com/

10 'The HeartMath Solution' page 72

11 https://www.stevefarber.com/books/

12 https://thestoryoftelling.com/books/

13 https://www.smartcompany.com.au/startupsmart/news/atlassian-remote-work-permanent/

14 https://www.druckerforum.org/blog/networks-are-not-communities-by-henry-mintzberg/

15 https://www.abc.net.au/news/2019-05-10/ben-elton-says-society-is-fracturing-with-manipulated-outrage/11097360

16 https://mintzberg.org/blog/communityship-beyond-leadership

17 https://therightcompany.co/

18 https://www.ianberry.biz/heart-leadership-village/

19 https://www.textpublishing.com.au/books/sand-talk

Sparkenation Three

Ask Your Head and Value Greatly The Minds of Others (Process Innovation)

"I do not fix problems. I fix my thinking.

Then problems fix themselves"

Louise L. Hay

Overview

Process innovation is the collaborative work of ensuring processes make it simple for people to bring their essence to their work. Process innovation is 21st century management.

Processes include policies, procedures, practices, philosophies, principles, structures and systems.

In this Sparkenation we're exploring:

- Why the purpose of process is making it simple for people to bring their essence to their work, the magic of methodologies and the excitement of enhancing the employee and customer experience.

- The context of being in an infinite game, value exchange and delivery, and the unbreakable links to living values and feeling valued.

- The game-changers of decision-making and problem-solving transparency, performance energetics, and checklists.

The purpose of process is making it simple for people to bring their essence to their work

"Simplicity is the ultimate form of sophistication."
Leonardo Da vinci

"Use best judgement in all situations" has been the one rule at Nordstrom for over one hundred years.

Nordstrom's employee manual says:

"We're glad to have you with our Company. Our number one goal is to provide outstanding customer service. Set both your personal and professional goals high. We have great confidence in your ability to achieve them.

Rule #1: Use best judgement in all situations. There are no additional rules. Please feel free to ask your department manager, store manager, or division general manager any question at any time."

If there was only one rule at your workplace what would it be?

I recommend taking considerable thinking time and energy to answer this question. Involve your employees, customers and other stakeholders.

After this consultation decide on your one rule.

Then begin to review and upgrade every process in your organisation in alignment with your one rule and the objective of making it simple for people to bring their essence to their work.

My one rule is not grand yet I find it profoundly effective. I'm seeking to see the essence in every person I have a conversation with and to reflect their one-of-a-kind significance back to them.

What's your one rule?

As you upgrade your processes to align with your one rule remember that processes include policies, procedures, practices, philosophies, principles, structures and systems.

Any misalignment and you will find that performance is less than what is possible.

I've been involved with over 1000 organisations in my thirty years working as a mentor. In every one of them at any given time there are seven great challenges:

1. Disagreement about the goal/direction/objective/aim/vision.

2. Disagreement about how best to achieve 1. above.

3. Assumption of agreement in 1. and/or 2., and a negative response when such assumptions result in perceived betrayal.

4. Confusion about who is doing precisely what and exactly where and when.

5. The value of output/s in relation to people's input/s is being questioned.

6. The strategy is too complex for most people to buy into.

7. There is no strategy or decision-making process.

Solutions to each of these challenges involve people (heart), process (head), and progress (hands).

The Magic of Methodology

Having a methodology enables us to think clearly about our work rather than focussing on outcomes

When things are not going according to plan with my client I visit two places to gain understanding of what's going on. Firstly I check to see that the business processes being followed mean it's simple for people to bring their best to their work. Secondly I find out if the methodologies being deployed are fit for purpose.

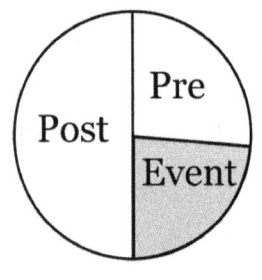

In 2005 I came across research completed in 2004 by Dr. Brent Peterson from Columbia University. He found that fifty percent of learning happens after an event and twenty-six percent prior to an event.

I have found that the consequences of applying this research have been profound for my clients. I can confidently guarantee to my clients that working together will mean a minimum 10 times return on their investment when they do the pre and post event work.

Routinely the following have become mandatory methodology for me:

As you consider my actions think about your own.

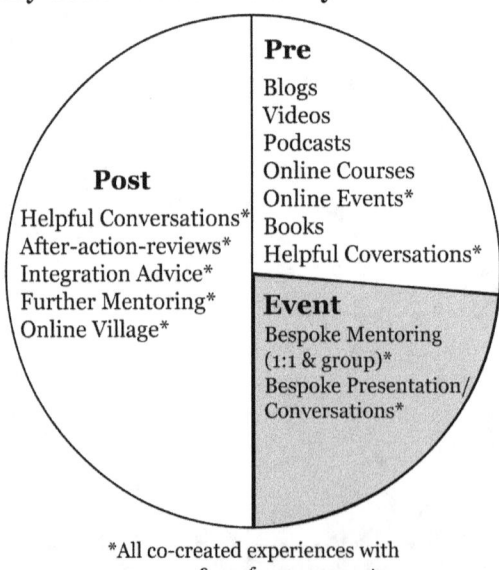

*All co-created experiences with peer group & performance partners

Pre

I email participants something to read, watch or listen to (or all three) from my blog relevant to the focus of the event.

I have a one to one conversation with participants to glean their understanding of what I have asked them to read, watch or listen to.

I carefully ask participants about their expectations prior to the event and what I can expect their levels of engagement to be.

Event

For me, events are primarily one to one or small group mentoring sessions, one to one or small group conversations, and presentation/conversations for up to thirty people.

Post

I email participants an audio recording of the event and resources for taking action (more read, watch and listen).

For private clients I will undertake an after-action-review.

After-action-reviews are a game-changer and a methodology themselves. This is because the only time to really effectively review performance is while every detail is still fresh in people's hearts and heads.

This is why all the great sports coaches get their teams in the room privately straight after the game and before they speak with anyone else.

Of course on the training track, during the week, videos are being reviewed to increase the value of immediate after-action reviews.

I recommend the following action for both informal and formal after-action-reviews and the integration work that follows:

1. Review one action at a time and answer the following questions What happened and why? What did we learn, relearn, and unlearn? How can we be better, wiser and more valuable in applying these learnings? Who will we become? What will we do next?
2. Determine with your colleagues how your answers will be integrated with what is already working well for you.

66 Heart Leadership

3. Upgrade individual, team and organisational plans-on-a-page accordingly.
4. Reflect new perceptions in the appropriate standard operating procedures, policies and practices.
5. Upgrade learning and development materials.

I also apply the pre and post methodology to other aspects of my work.

Regardless of the "event" I am taking my clients on a journey from information to insight (pre) to inspiration to idea/s (event) to implementation to introspection to integration to innovation (post). This too is a methodology.

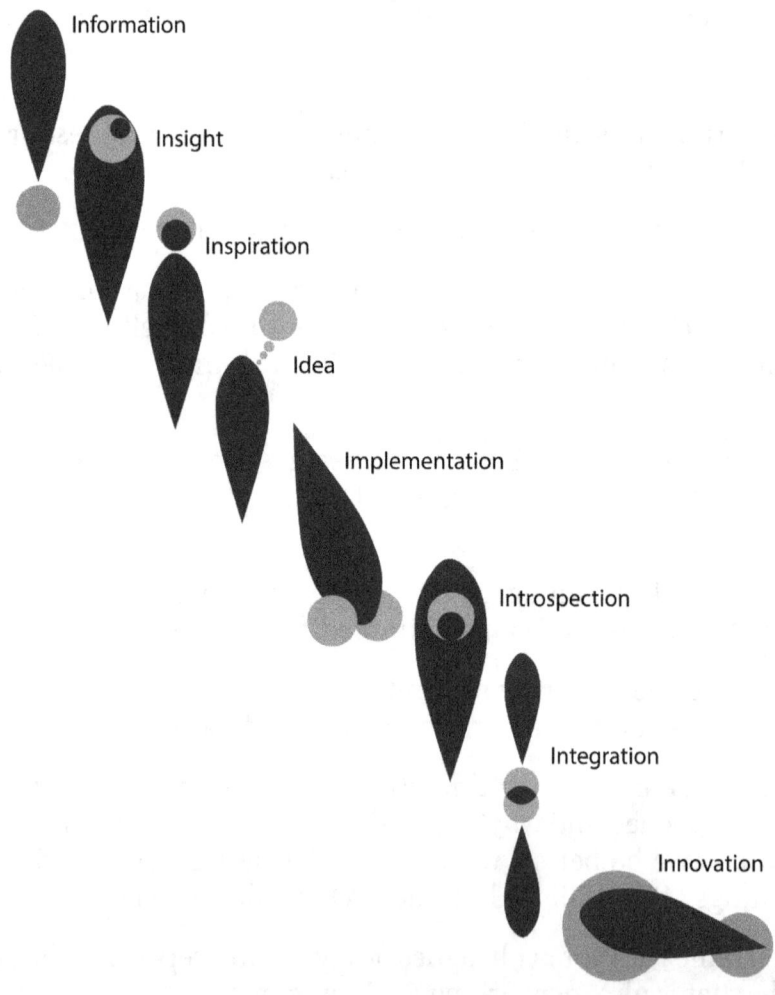

Let's take a look at each phase:

Information

Information is everywhere. We're drowning in it. It's accessible and mostly free. Deliberate distribution of disinformation is now rife. One of the challenges today is determining whether information is true or false. The bottom-line, information is actually of very little value. What we crave is insight.

Insight

Insight is the value, to you and other people, of information. It's what resonates in our hearts in the moment.

Determining insight is a most worthy pursuit because it's the beginning of more people feeling valued, living values and delivering and exchanging value, which are the fundamentals of a thriving enterprise.

Inspiration

Very few people take the time and energy to savour insight and imagine what can be. To be inspired, heart is required. Emotions need stirring.

Idea/s

Any idea from the heart, inspired by intuition, is worthy of consideration. There's three key questions to answer:

1. What's your process for considering people's ideas and getting back to them once considered?
2. What is the decision-making process for choosing an idea to implement?
3. How much freedom do your people have to implement ideas?

Then love your idea like your dearest. Find people who love it too. Work with them to turn your idea into innovation through the final three crucial stages.

Implementation

There are three essentials for successfully implementing any idea.

1. Do so in one quantum leap (i.e. small yet significant step) at a time.

2. Implement in ninety day blocks using performance possibility plans-on-a-page. Ninety days is enough time to do things that matter and yet short enough to be able to correct any missteps.

3. Aggregate the marginal gains.

We will explore the above in detail in the next Sparkenation about Progress Sustainability.

Introspection

To reflect on actions taken and their impact is vital to all learning and progress of any kind. I help a lot of my clients with after-action-reviews and have a simple five stage process as referenced previously.

Integration

Integrating new perceptions with what is already working well for you is an essential to embedding learning and establishing new levels of performance.

The best way that I know of to carry out integration work is as per the five stage process mentioned above.

Innovation

Innovation has occurred when we have changed what's normal, when we have shifted from sameness or the status quo, that was no longer serving us, to something more valuable.

Conversations are the glue that sustain methodology and also enable continuous improvement

Sparkenation conversations have become my trademark and my main methodology in my work with clients as well as my online events.

Remember a Sparkenation is *"a spark that ignites passion that leads to action that changes what's normal."*

My promise is that Sparkenation Conversations will contain these wonderful ingredients:

1. Safe, peer group environment.

2. High energy.

3. Candid, convivial, compassionate, conscious, and compelling conversation.

4. Humour.

5. Prominence given to curiosity, sense of wonder and generosity.

6. Heart stirring and thought shifting moments.

7. Relevant, timely, immediately usable content that is also highly valuable in the long term.

8. Leads you to small yet significant shifts (quantum leaps) you decide to make in your own best way.

Through many hours of my own after-action-reviews and integration work I have noticed that, to fulfil this promise, there are twenty-four components that we must ensure come into play during a conversation.

I call them The Sparkenation Conversation Essentials. I list them below.

Love	Gratitude	Self-awareness	Awareness of others
Being in the room	Playing your role	Questioning	Listening to understand
Noticing	Appreciation	Curiosity	Openness
Compassion	Essentialism	Kindness	Generosity
Care	Silence	Epiphany/ defining moments	Shared view in the seven areas of significance
Harmony	Happiness	People first, environment second, profit last	Best version of you inspiring the best version of me

Earlier we explored the heart qualities of love, gratitude, appreciation, care, happiness, compassion, harmony, kindness.

We have also referenced my belief that self-awareness is the number one leadership skill and awareness of others the second.

And we know the high value of everyone 'playing your role' which is my twenty-first century language for being accountable.

Let's examine the others:

Being in the room

Legendary United Kingdom based professional speaker and author Nigel Risner says *"when you're in the room, be in the room"*.

It is easy to get distracted, particularly online. We are doing each other a disservice though, when we are not giving our undivided attention.

I was reminded of this once, many years ago, when a colleague, whose opinion I still seek out and highly regard, suggested to me, after coming to hear me speak, that I gave a great presentation yet let people down because I wasn't really in the room before hand. Ouch. I have been in the room every time since!

Questioning

Heart-Leaders are admired for the questions they ask, more than the answers they give to other people's questions.

Listening to understand

Understanding the feelings of a fellow human being and engaging in feeling talk is a great gift we give others as well as ourselves. Sharing feelings is heart language. It's very different to usual conversation which is about opinions and facts or what people perceive as facts which are actually opinions!

Noticing

A wise mentor of mine once told me that giving a gift was not as important as the words on the card. I have never forgotten this.

Curiosity

I am fortunate that I was born curious. I'm curious first about people. Everyone we meet is a one-of-a-kind human being. The silent question I am always asking is *"What's special about this one-of-a-kind in front of me?"*

I'm also curious about process. I'm always considering *"How does this work? How could this work better for people?"*

I'm curious about unchanging principles too and how I can apply them and how I can help others to apply them in their own best way.

Openness

The ability to hold opposing views in our minds at once was regarded by the writer F. Scott Fitzgerald as a sign of first rate intelligence.

I believe in social democracy, for example, and lean to the left.

Therefore I need to understand the right and other forms of democracy and how different views are opposed to mine in order to sustain an open heart and head.

I do not believe in right or wrong or in any particular way being better than another. What I'm searching for is a shared-view and how to collaborate with other people who may have fundamentally different beliefs to mine.

Essentialism

I invested a year (2015) in studying 'essentialism'[1] and its central idea of "less but better". Living this concept has been transformational for me and for those I have supported as they adopt it.

Generosity

I love this wonderful line from the founder of Wired Magazine, Kevin Kelly *"Optimize your generosity. No one on their deathbed has ever regretted giving too much away."*

I have found that the more I give without attachment to getting back the more I get back.

Silence

I have come to recognise that wonderful words of inspiration and ideas that take your breath away often follow moments of silence. I once waited eleven minutes after posing a question to a group. The most inexperienced person in the room was the first to speak and her words changed us all forever.

Epiphany/defining moments

There's nothing quite like it, is there, when the penny drops for someone? Witnessing other people's 'ah ha' moments always gives me joy.

Significance of shared-view in the seven areas of significance

When there is a shared-view of these significant seven in any team, desired results happen.

1. Where you are (reality),
2. Where you're going (possibility),
3. Why you're going there (purpose),
4. How you will get there (strategy),
5. Who will do what and when (execution),
6. How you will know you are on track (progress),
7. How you will behave along the way (culture and values).

The magnificent seven are explored in detail in 'The Appreciative Leader' handbook which you can download from the one PDF that contains links to all my digital resources and online courses.[2]

People first, environment second, profit last

The biggest emotional and spiritual losers in life, I have observed, are those who put profit before people and the planet.

There is nothing wrong or evil about making money. Profit, I believe, is a result of being good at business. It can never be a reason for being in business. And it can never be made at the expense of people or our planet.

Best version of you inspiring the best version of me

My friend and colleague Matt Church says *"Leadership is about making sure the best version of you speaks to the best version of us."*

This is at the core of Heart-Leadership, seeking the best version in people, process and progress.

Each of these twenty-four Sparkenation Conversation Essentials creates a natural energy flow from heart to head to hands.

The excitement of enhancing the employee and customer experience

The future of your business is all about your humanity, how you see and treat people.

Then you can concern yourself with how technology can help you to enable and enhance the experience you provide for your employees and customers/clients.

I carry an umbrella in the bottom of my briefcase. I have only ever been stopped at an airport once. The security person on that day went way over the top when my bag went through the security device with my umbrella in it.

On the return I thought I would avoid unnecessary delay and rudeness by taking my umbrella out of my briefcase. The security guy said *"No need mate thank you, our equipment picks them up easily."* Same equipment, different response. One guy rude, one guy pleasant.

Why the inconsistency? I suspect it has much to do with the employee experience.

The best future of your business depends greatly on how remarkable the experience of your employees and therefore the customer experience which flows from the employee experience.

The very best employee and customer experience begins with four actions:

1. Role clarity and recruiting people to match roles.
2. How well your processes make it simple for your employees to bring their essence to their work.
3. Ensuring your employees are fully equipped to provide memorable service.
4. How empowered your employees are to use their initiative and create an awesome experience for other people.

Employee and Customer Experience expert, Paul Schmeja, the CEO of First Contact, worked at the Melbourne 2006 Commonwealth Games.

Paul says. *"I was due to commence in early January, I remember getting a call from my soon to be manager, just before Christmas, simply wishing me a Happy Christmas and how much they were looking forward to me joining the team in the new-year.*

On my first day, like any new employee, I approached Reception around 9am on a Monday to present myself. What immediately impressed and surprised me was that I was expected! The Receptionist knew the names of the dozen or so new starters for that day, and ushered us into the room for induction. Later in the day, when I was taken to my department and shown to my new desk. My name was already on the workstation, top drawer filled with brand-new stationary, my computer log-on details, and a box of business cards already printed.

The first impression, that I was an anticipated, valued member of the team, set the tone for a very successful chapter in my career.

I have made it a point to treat employees in my care as the "first customer". This translates to team members who feel valued, looked after and will, in turn, do their best to make your customers feel valued and looked after."

If I was beginning employment at your place what would my first day be like? If I came to your place what would my experience be like as a customer?

I have experienced great service in person from one organisation and lousy service from the same organisation online.

Would I find your levels of service online and in person to be different?

The service experience we provide our customers/clients with and indeed co-create with them, matters more than ever.

Everywhere you look there are headlines saying The Future of Business Is Technology.

What if it isn't?

All day, every day there's talk of digital revolution and disruption. What if this isn't what really matters?

In her wonderful book 'Meaningful: The Story of Ideas That Fly', Bernadette Jiwa says:

"... it's not the technology in isolation, particular platforms or specialised functionality that's driving the change; what's driving this new wave of relevance is the humanity of the entrepreneurs and business owners who create the products and user experiences that people love."

I couldn't agree more.

What about you?

The future of your business is all about your humanity, how you see and treat people. Then you can concern yourself with how technology can help you to enable and enhance the experience you provide for your customers/clients.

Steve Jobs was onto this long ago of course. He said *"You've got to start with the customer experience and work backwards to the technology."*

To get excited I highly recommend heart and head work as follows:

1. Undertake extensive review of your client/customer experience. What is it truly like? How could it be better? Of course it goes without saying that you would ask your customers these questions!

2. Look at every transaction and interaction with clients/customers. What improvements could be made in light of the answers to 1. above.

3. Overall what is the level of employee satisfaction? Ask them of course. And take action accordingly.

Turning Possibility Into Reality - further suggested actions

- Continually review whether everyone you work with understands that communication has occurred when two or more people have reached a shared-view regarding the way to move forward together, or not. Please remember that communication is not information sharing, soundbites, tweets, LinkedIn or Facebook updates, or any social media posts, advertising or press releases.

- Refresh your listening skills so that you improve your understanding of what is being said (content), why it's meaningful for the person/people (context), and what that is really about (concept).

- Take at least one course every year to improve your ability to share stories other people can see and feel themselves in. Humour that is self-deprecating is common in these stories. Get better at this too.

- Say what you feel more often.

- Make it clear when you are sharing your opinion and what you believe to be a fact.

- With your peers create a methodology for confronting disinformation (what we call BS in Aussie speak), and helping people to humanely remove warts, skeletons in closets, and elephants from boardrooms, offices, factories and shops. Make sure your methodology is convivial i.e. cordial, cheerful, friendly, good natured and good-humoured.

- Review what happens before and after your events (meetings, conversations, learning and development sessions, whatever). How will you be more human as well as more efficient and effective?

Do Your Work.

When we're all playing an infinite game

A finite game has the purpose of winning, meaning the game ends once there's a winner or winners.

An infinite game is played with the purpose of continuing the game.

With gratitude to James P. Carse and Simon Sinek.

I'm long done with winning and competition. Instead I'm focused on continuity and collaboration.

I still compete with myself.

I'm long past trying to compete with other people. Friendly games of golf or chess etc are the exception.

Life is much more joyful and enjoyable when my focus is on being the best version of me.

There's no need for comparison or competition anyway of course because each of us is a one-of-a-kind human being.

A finite game has the purpose of winning, meaning the game ends once there's a winner or winners.

An infinite game is played with the purpose of continuing the game.

An infinite game is a much more curious and interesting game. We will explore this more in the Sparkenation about progress.

Consider the damage that the finite game of economic growth has done to our world particularly post GFC (Global Financial Crisis) and DC (during coronavirus) and AC (after coronavirus).

Remember the one rule we explored earlier.

In many Western governments the one rule is economic growth and therefore decisions made in GFC times and DC and AC were fundamentally flawed because we were looking at everything through an economic lens rather than equally through social, environmental, spiritual and universal lenses.

The infinite game is about value exchange and delivery

"Do not try to become a person of success

but try to become a person of value."

Attributed to Albert Einstein

What is your value promise to each of your various stakeholder relationships and how well are you currently fulfilling these promises?

Many organisational structures are too complicated to be able to effectively answer this question. Usually the problems are an outcome of command and control management where one or more individuals want to be involved in everything and can't or won't let go of decision-making.

I love the work of German author and advisor Niels Pflaeging[3]. Niels believes that every organisation has three structures, formal, informal and what he calls value creation structure. It's this one that I'm particularly interested in here.

The keys to value creation for me are roles, relationships and what value is demanded, desired and felt deserved, and what is actually being delivered to and exchanged with people.

We have already touched on aspects of these when we explored role clarity statements.

Value, like beauty, is in the eyes of the beholder.

What are the key relationships in your workplace?

Most likely there are seven to carefully consider:

1. Employees with customers/clients.
2. Employees with other employees.
3. Employees with employers.
4. Employees with external suppliers.
5. Employees with other stakeholders.

6. Employees within communities where your workplace operates.

7. Employers within such communities.

I highly recommend repeating the Value Exchange and Delivery Refresh exercise below that we referenced earlier only this time take into account each of the seven above.

	Relationships	Task and Transactions	The Experience
Must Receive			
Should Receive			
Nice to Receive			

Giver: Receiver:
Date:

Value is the glue that binds together living values and feeling valued

Employee/Employer Value Promise or EEVP

In the thriving modern enterprise people feel valued, live values and deliver and exchange value. The latter is the glue that binds together living values and feel valued.

An Employee/Employer Value Promise or EEVP can play a role.

EEVP's replace the old world of work vision, mission and values statements. Such statements were often propositions and were seen as platitudes and so are long past their use by dates. You can even Google ones to adopt. This is a sure-fire way to perish in the modern organisation. In fact I say a cut and paste of anything has inherent danger. Whatever you do make it bespoke.

EEVP's are defined by the word promise. Keep the promise regardless of situations and your trust levels will increase.

Break your promise and people will leave you, or worse stay with you and not do their best work.

I highly recommend creating an EEVP with your employees. My warning is only do so if you are going to keep the promise no matter what happens.

What would be in such a promise?

Please consider the following five vital aspects:

1. What happens when mistakes are made? Do you ask who did it or what happened?
2. What are the agreed behaviours of your values? Words are fine, behaviour is what actually matters.
3. Keep your promise to no more than one page.
4. Ask your employees to co-create your EEVP with you. We don't feel as if we own what is handed down. We do feel ownership when we have been engaged in the creation.

5. Agree on how trusting one another is lived.

What would you consider vital?

Invoke the key catalysts of the head

The following catalysts are crucial to delivering and exchanging value:

Openness

This is one of the twenty-four Sparkenation Conversation Essentials.

From a thinking perspective openness means avoiding bias and suspending ideologies and beliefs and being completely open to the unlimited possibilities every moment offers.

Such openness is a foundation stone of Heart-Leadership.

Sense-making

"Sensemaking or sense-making is the process by which people give meaning to their collective experiences. It has been defined as "the ongoing retrospective development of plausible images that rationalize what people are doing"[4]

The key for me is giving meaning. A wonderful habit to nurture is exploring with folk what they mean and what has meaning for them.

Such sense-making is a foundation stone of Heart-Leadership.

Decision-making

We will address this formally in the section on transparency coming up next. For now, see it as a process that helps others to see how you thought through something or arrived at the decision you did. This is a great giving meaning to something action within itself.

Such decision-making is a foundation stone of Heart-Leadership.

Problem-solving

Asking people you meet "What problems do you solve?" Or my preference "What challenges do you help other people to overcome?" are much more intriguing questions than "So what do you do?"

Like decision-making, problem-solving that is transparent and has meaning helps us all to think clearly and to fully utilise our mind's amazing capacity to provide us with how to's.

Such problem-solving is a foundation stone of Heart-Leadership.

Imagination

The following is from Albert Einstein's 1931 published book "Cosmic Religion and Other Opinions and Aphorisms'

"At times I feel certain I am right while not knowing the reason. When the eclipse of 1919 confirmed my intuition, I was not in the least surprised. In fact, I would have been astonished had it turned out otherwise. Imagination is more important than knowledge. For knowledge is limited, whereas imagination embraces the entire world, stimulating progress, giving birth to evolution. It is, strictly speaking, a real factor in scientific research."

I love *"For knowledge is limited, whereas imagination embraces the entire world, stimulating progress, giving birth to evolution."*

John Lennon of course was onto this insight in his wonderful anthem 'Imagine'.

> *"Imagine there's no countries*
>
> *It isn't hard to do*
>
> *Nothing to kill or die for*
>
> *And no religion, too*
>
> *Imagine all the people*
>
> *Living life in peace*
>
> *You, you may say I'm a dreamer*
>
> *But I'm not the only one*
>
> *I hope someday you will join us*
>
> *And the world will be as one ..."*

Such imagination is a foundation stone of Heart-Leadership.

Human-centred design

I'm a fan of the people at IDEO, the global design company. In their Field Guide to Human Centered Design, they say, *"When you understand the people you're trying to reach—and then design from their perspective—not only will you arrive at unexpected answers, but you'll come up with ideas that they'll embrace."*

I only do bespoke work with Enthusiasts for this reason. I'm meticulous in my research with the goal of understanding the people I'm working with. The work is then all about them applying proven principles in their own best way.

Such human-centred design is a foundation stone of Heart-Leadership.

Systems-thinking

I'm always interested in how humans interact and transact with other humans as well as with technology. Any technology that doesn't enhance the human experience is of no interest to me.

Heart-Leaders are asking how does this feel or how could this feel? before engaging the head to work out system changes.

Such systems-thinking is a foundation stone of Heart-Leadership.

Curiosity

Curiosity is also one of the 24 Sparkenation Conversation Essentials previously referenced. From a thinking perspective, being curious is paying attention to the human experience and thinking about how things can be different, better or more valuable from a human perspective.

Such curiosity is a foundation stone of Heart-Leadership.

The following is the flow of each of these from the eight heart qualities to the corresponding head catalysts:

Heart Qualities	Head Catalysts
Love	Openness
Gratitude	Sense-making
Appreciation	Decision-making
Care	Problem-solving
Happiness	Imagination
Compassion	Human centred design
Harmony	Systems thinking
Kindness	Curiosity

Turning Possibility Into Reality - further suggested actions

- Reflect and describe what you believe is the game you're playing or changing. Is it a finite game or an infinite game?
- Then have a conversation with stakeholders in your life and work about what they believe is the game you're playing.
- Notice the language being used in the above.
- What changes/modifications/nuances will you make to how you describe who you are and what you bring to the world?
- Be of service to others by offering to be engaged with them in the above actions.
- Reflect on your flow from heart qualities to head catalysts. In what ways will you increase flow and reduce struggle, uncertainty or scarcity.

Do Your Work.

The game-changer of decision-making and problem-solving transparency

Our lives are a consequence of the choices and decisions we make and don't make.

The right decisions made at the right time by the people in the best position to make them is what everybody wants.

In reality, and the first problem, is that at least half the decisions made by business people are not the best decisions that could be made.

These were the findings of two decades of research by Dr Paul Nutt of Ohio State University and involving hundreds of organisations. The research found that there are three key reasons why 50% of decisions fail:

1. *"One third driven by ego.*
2. *Nearly two thirds of executives never explore alternatives once they make up their mind.*
3. *Eighty percent of managers push their decisions through by persuasion or edict and not by the value of their idea."*

The second big problem that I see is Lack of Transparency

For BIG decisions never make a decision until all the angles have been thoroughly viewed and debated.

Have a process.

Following is the process that I give to my clients to get them started when they don't have their own, which is sadly, usually the case.

Having a process means transparency of decision making which means greater acceptance and higher support for your decisions.

Having a process also means a greater likelihood of

- Buy-in by those affected by the decision.
- Higher probability of making the right decision.
- Less poor decisions.
- Less decisions You need to make in the first place!

Ask Your Head 87

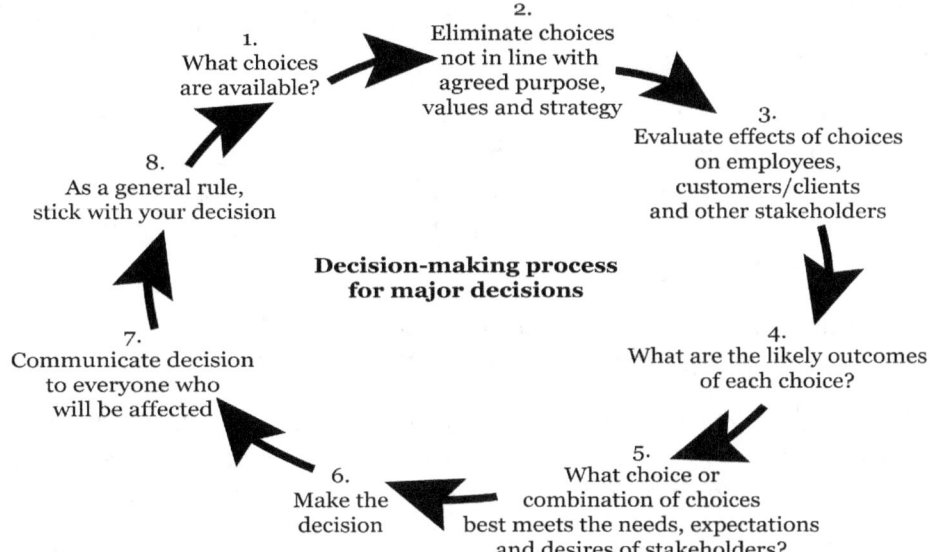

My colleague and resident of The Heart-Leadership Online Village, Simone Boer, led a remarkable community engagement project for her employer The City of Greater Geelong. It provides great insight into the power of transparency to engage people. Here is Simone' story:

"*Historically, Geelong's identity has been firmly entrenched in manufacturing being the home to Ford, Shell, Alcoa, the Port.*

The early 2010's signalled a difficult time in Geelong as the very foundation on which the region has been built was closing it's doors. Many workers found themselves without a job. When people and the media spoke about the region, it was often portrayed in a negative light.

In 2016, 'Our Future', a strengths based engagement with the community designed to build the mental wealth of the community and develop a community-led vision was run.

The Our Future engagement was designed to capture the potential of the community of Geelong, understand their aspirations and have a positive engagement with each and every person who shared their voice.

The result was Greater Geelong: A Clever and Creative Future, a thirty year community vision that bought together the voices of over 16,000 people, reached an audience of 750,000 nationally, across

180,000 data points in 170+ workshops, events, shopping centre visits and mailouts.

Since the launch of the Clever and Creative Vision for Geelong, the community has come to own the vision as evidenced by everyday conversations, references within local media, local businesses aligning their plans to the aspirations of the vision and designation by UNESCO as a City of Design.

The engagement that resulted in the development of Geelong's vision is the largest local engagement completed nationally.

Because the vision contains the voices of so many community members, it is the community who are now working in partnership with businesses and government to celebrate it and bring it to life.

Although only three years old, Clever and Creative has now become a part of the narrative of Geelong and is now interwoven with the positivity and identity of the region."

The third problem I see is leaders unnecessarily involving themselves in decisions where they shouldn't be

If this is happening at your business carry out a review as soon as practical to ensure that every day decisions are being made by the people doing the work and who are involved in customer/client transactions and interactions.

Make sure that people are genuinely empowered to make decisions and that you have clarity with them about how they will be held to account.

Every day there are opportunities to innovate

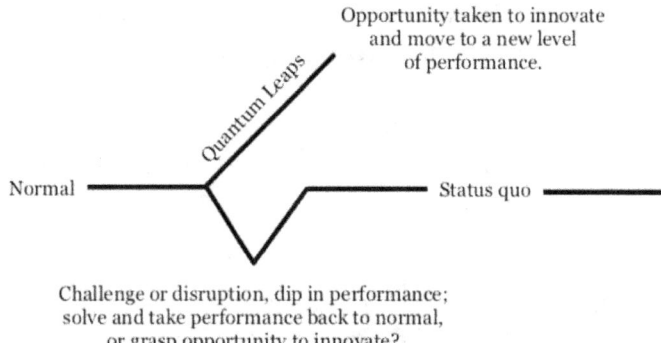

with thanks to Alan Weiss whose work inspired me to create this model.

The above becomes an every day innovation enabler which, of course, is key to process innovation.

The straight line in the above diagram represents what is normal practice in the majority of organisations. Be the exception and take the quantum leap route.

There's a lot of talk about 'disruptive innovation'. The biggest disruption we need to make often is to disrupt ourselves and to change the status quo when sameness is no longer serving us.

Quantum leaps are often thought of as big jumps. They are in fact small yet significant shifts. More about this in the Hands Sparkenation.

Decision-making structures and systems like those referred to above are a key part of ensuring that management of your processes mean it is simple for your people to bring their essence to their work every day.

And remember processes include policies, procedures, practices, philosophies, principles, structures and systems.

The game-changer of performance energetics

People don't want to be appraised.
We want to be appreciated.

Performance Energetics is my alternative to performance appraisals and formal performance reviews. I believe people want autonomy and freedom to do their best work. Typical appraisals and performance reviews are an impediment.

People are happy to work within agreed boundaries. The last thing we want though is a feeling we're being controlled.

Controlling people and compliance are the usual intents behind traditional performance appraisals and performance review systems. This is why most people hate them so much.

I still come across organisations doing performance appraisals even though there is a mountain of evidence (just Google it) that says they are bad for people and that they create bad energy, let alone of course bad blood.

Appraising people in my view is a dehumanising and de-harmonising waste of energy, and it may even scar people almost beyond healing.

As I say

People don't want to be appraised.

We want to be appreciated.

This doesn't mean that we don't want to be questioned or held to account when we fall short of our best selves. The issue is how this happens and the intent behind the call out.

Energetics, in simple terms, means energy quality. Performance Energetics is about sustaining high energy and flow.

Often following Heart-Leadership work I help my clients to upgrade their performance review system, including eliminating performance appraisals.

From a Heart-Leadership perspective the premise is that we should agree with people about the outcomes or outputs of their work, let them do their work however they wish within the boundaries of other agreements, while engaging with them in an ongoing conversation.

We will explore conversation more in the Hands Sparkenation.

For now the following insight by poet and leadership expert David Whyte says it all:

> *"In leadership the conversation isn't about the work, the conversation is the work."*

Performance Energetics provides a framework for such conversations to be meaningful and valuable for all.

Performance Energetics is about attracting, on-boarding, engaging, retaining people and wisdom, and remaining respectful when we part company.

Performance Energetics is also about who is doing the work much more than where or when the work is being done.

The future of work is very much about alignment and sustaining shared-view in the seven areas of significance (reality, possibility, purpose, strategy, execution, progress and culture) wherever people may be located physically and virtually.

Below is an overview of each of the components. In the Hands Sparkenation we will delve into the actions that make them reality.

Attracting

Attention today is a precious gift. We all want people paying attention to us. As with most of the important matters in life, 'we get what we give'.

We earn attention by being people of value.

The five essentials are:

- Remarkable relationships with existing employees for they are the greatest source of new employees.

- Having an employee bank (a list of people we have already vetted, have a relationship with, and who we know are right for our organisation).

- Role clarity statements.
- Easily verifiable credibility and reputation in the marketplace.
- A remarkable culture (the behaviours you live by and how you go about your work, and being role models in people leadership, 'Hear Your Heart', Sparkenation Two).

On-boarding

In my first job the only induction was being told by my supervisor *"morning tea is at 10 am, lunch 12 pm, you eat in here and can put your personal stuff there. Keep your head down, do what you're told and mind your own business. Tools down at 3 pm every day."*

Sadly in many workplaces not much has changed.

Today, to properly and professionally onboard people, we must:

- Compete all agreed paperwork that would include the Employer/Employee Promise (EEVP), their contract of employment, all documents that protect their rights and yours including their safety and well-being, as well as all documents required by your laws.
- Arrange meetings in the first two weeks with everyone the person's role has relationships with to agree on value exchange and delivery.
- Take people through decision-making and problem solving processes and systematically work through all other standard operating processes (remember these include policies, procedures, practices, principles, philosophies, systems and frameworks).
- Explain and agree on protocols for safety, well-being, communication and conversations internally and externally including the media.
- Reinforce your remarkable culture (the behaviours you live by and how you go about your work, and being role models in people leadership, 'Hear Your Heart', Sparkenation Two), as well as linking to aspects in this 'Ask Your Head' Process Innovation Sparkenation.

Engaging

People will feel valued, live values and exchange and deliver value (all three mean engaged) as a consequence of the effectiveness of their on-boarding. From there it's a matter of sustainability. The keys are:

- Daily conversations that sustain shared-view in the seven areas of significance, namely reality, possibility, purpose, strategy, execution, progress and culture.[5]
- Openness and transparency modelled through a legitimate open door policy.
- Having places available for private and confidential conversation.
- Ongoing learning and development opportunities that enable people to continue to learn, grow and contribute.
- Reinforce your remarkable culture (the behaviours you live by and how you go about your work, and being role models in people leadership, 'Hear Your Heart', Sparkenation Two), as well as linking to aspects in this 'Ask Your Head', Process Innovation Sparkenation.

Retaining people and wisdom

When your daily conversations enable the twenty-four essentials of Sparkenation Conversations below on a consistent basis you will both retain people and wisdom (assuming people are achieving agreed outcomes or outputs and are happy overall).

Below is a reminder of the twenty-four essentials:

Love	Gratitude	Self-awareness	Awareness of others
Being in the room	Playing your role	Questioning	Listening to understand
Noticing	Appreciation	Curiosity	Openness
Compassion	Essentialism	Kindness	Generosity
Care	Silence	Epiphany/ defining moments	Shared view in the seven areas of significance

Harmony	Happiness	People first, environment second, profit last	Best version of you inspiring the best version of me

Here are five further success elements:

- Praise people in public, offer critique (when requested or as part of an agreement) in private.
- Acknowledge work, reward behaviours and agreed outcomes/outputs.
- Encourage and role-model sharing of lessons learned from failing and not quite getting there.
- Remember everyone is doing their best and infuse this into your behaviour and language.
- Reinforce your remarkable culture (the behaviours you live by and how you go about your work, and being role models in people leadership, 'Hear Your Heart', Sparkenation Two), as well as linking to aspects in this 'Ask Your Head', Process Innovation Sparkenation.

Remaining respectful when you part company (in the old world of work we called this Succession Planning)

Once upon a time people worked for the one organisation their entire lives.

In my corporate career which ended thirty years ago I worked for four corporations over a seventeen year period. This was considered unusual.

Today people can work for several organisations at once and even when they are feeling valued, living values and exchanging and delivering value still may part company with you.

Here are five guidelines for retaining a high value and mutually rewarding relationship:

- Be open and transparent with people about career options and have them work to ensure someone is ready to replace them in their role when they leave. The Career and Life-Calling Card, coming up in the section about checklists, is a great way to help with this.

- Support people in going for interviews with other organisations. Our role as Heart-Leaders is always to be supportive of people in finding their happy place.

- In daily conversations with people incorporate stories and lessons from the past, what's happening now and what can be in the future.

- Stay in touch with people when they move to another organisation. Perhaps provide forums. Create some kind of fraternity or alumni.

- Reinforce your remarkable culture (the behaviours you live by and how you go about your work, and being role models in people leadership, 'Hear Your Heart', Sparkenation Two), as well as linking to aspects in this 'Ask Your Head', Process Innovation Sparkenation, and the Engage Your Hands, Progress Sustainabiity Sparkenation coming up soon.

In the section on checklists that follows I provide a further 25 ways to move from performance management to Performance Energetics.

The game-changer of checklists

Checklists not only enhance living they can also save lives.

In the acknowledgments section there are several books that I highly recommend you read.

One of these is the 'The Checklist Manifesto: How to Get Things Right' by medical doctor Atul Gawande[6]. In this book he wonderfully illustrates how checklists save lives.

DC (during coronavirusvirus) following a checklist has saved lives.

I'm sure you've seen a version of the following

- Wash your hands often.
- Avoid close contact.
- Cover your mouth and nose with a cloth face cover when around others.
- Cover coughs and sneezes.
- Clean and disinfect.
- Monitor Your Health Daily.

Once not even doctors washed their hands. As the good doctor points out in his book this cost many lives. Importantly doctors adopting the practice as routine has saved many lives.

In operating theatres a leader calls time out to check that everything is in place and all instruments etc. are accounted for. This simple checklist has saved many lives and many pre and post operation disasters.

In my work I use checklists for many things to ensure that I never leave anything important or vital out of interactions and transactions. I encourage my clients to adopt checklists as a matter of normal practice. Many report the well-being impact on people as well as financial savings and rewards.

Helpful Conversations

My friend and colleague and best-selling author Bernadette Jiwa reckons marketing is simply a series of 'helpful conversations'. I love this concept.

At the beginning of 2020 I resolved never to sell in the old world way ever again. Since then I have focused on giving value (books, online courses and digital resources), demonstrating value (one-of-a-kind live online events), and living my value (having helpful conversations).

Here's my checklist for ensuring all my conversations are helpful:

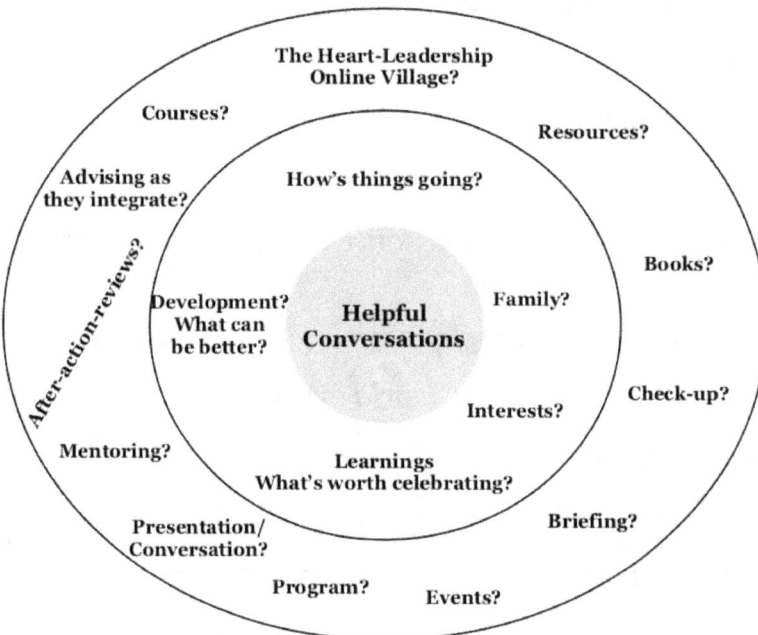

In all my helpful conversations with clients, colleagues and people interested in my work my first focus is always on other people and their circumstances, dreams, hopes and aspirations (the inner circle).

If there's a flow and a natural rhythm then I may explore the items in the outer circle with people.

I have this checklist on my desk or wherever I am when I make the calls to make sure I don't miss anything of value.

The Future Manifesto

'The Future Manifesto, 10 guiding principles for co-creating a positive future' is an ongoing project I am engaged in with colleagues from The Right Company.[7]

Manifestos make great checklists.

I use The Future Manifesto in a number of ways. One way is to choose one or more of the 10 guiding principles as an overarching theme for my work over a set period of time. For example while writing this book (June - November 2020) I chose principles 1., 4. and 7. (see below).

So every morning before beginning to write I check-in with these three principles and align my intention through hearing my heart and then asking my head. I then engage my hands and write.

"The 10 guiding principles

1. *Focus on inspiration more than motivation.*
2. *Jump from competition to collaboration.*
3. *See what emerges when you dance with fear, ambiguity, and not-knowing.*
4. *Discover the inner energy of your breath and your heart.*
5. *Your health and that of the world are one.*
6. *Start your mission to be kinder than necessary.*
7. *Create something humanity really needs.*
8. *Move from measurement into the universe of possibility.*
9. *Join the infinite game and become a compass and guiding star.*
10. *Take this as a time of opportunities, unique in our history."*

The Career and Life-Calling Card

Discovering our life's work is one of the most fulfilling quests we can achieve. I recommend creating a checklist like The Career and Life-Calling Card below and reviewing it at least twice a year to see where you're at and where you could move to.

According to Gallup and many other leading researchers into employee engagement, most of the world's employees are not fully engaged in their work.

There are many reasons for this disaster.

Often overlooked is the fact that millions of people aren't able or allowed to do what they love in the service of people who love what they do. Hence they're disengaged. A Career and Life-Calling Card helps.

I'm am very grateful to the works of Joseph Campbell, Ken Robinson, Steven Farber, Daniel Pink, and Hector Garcia and Francesc Miralles for their work in the area of vocation/work/mission/purpose.

You'll find their books listed in the Acknowledgements Section.

The concept of *"Follow your bliss"* comes from Joseph Campbell in his book 'Hero of a thousand faces'. It has resonated with me since I first read the book over 30 years ago.

The very best explanation that I have ever come across for *"follow your bliss"* comes from the film 'Finding Joe'[8] which is a documentary about Joseph Campbell's work.

In the film the President of the Joseph Campbell Foundation describes bliss as *"doing what you can't not do."* I love this!

In an excellent book 'The Element - how finding your passion changes everything', Ken Robinson[9] says about the element *"the place where the things we love to do and the things we are good at come together."*

"Do what you love, in the service of people who love what you do." says Steven Farber in 'The Radical Leap'. This is perhaps my favourite line of all time when it comes to meaningful work.

What drives us according to Daniel Pink in his books, 'A Whole New Mind' and 'Drive - the surprising truth about what motivates us.' Is the three factors below:

"Autonomy: the urge to direct our own lives.

Mastery: the desire to get better and better at something that matters.

Purpose: the yearning to do what we do in the service of something larger than ourselves."

The Japanese say everyone has an ikigai. The French call it raison d'etre.

In their beautiful book 'Ikigai The Japanese Secret to a Long and

Happy Life', Hector Garcia and Francesc Miralles quote from people born in Okinawa, the island with the most centenarians in the world - *"our ikigai is the reason we get up in the morning."*

All of these works and my own experience in working with people to find their essence I conclude that our life's work, our reasons for being, is found at the intersection between Can do, Will do, Love to do, and People who love what I do.

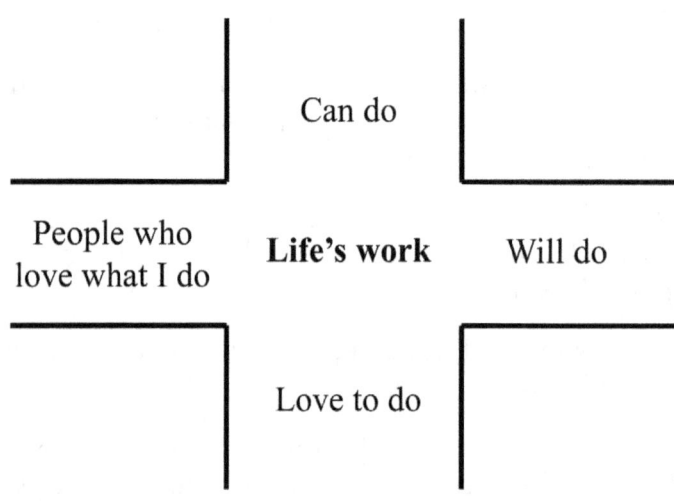

I recommend creating a one-page visual as a key heart and head action.

Career and Life-Calling Card where you would feature your answers the following questions:

Can Do

What do I know?

What are my key skills?

What is my real expertise?

How do I practice what I know?

Will do

What is my attitude to living?

What am I really committed to?

How can I be more disciplined in taking action?

How I am really different from others who do what I do?

Love to do

My purpose in life is?

I am passionate about?

I find Joy in?

My art is?

My essence is?

People who love what I do

How do I:

Serve others?

Help people achieve what is important to them?

Solve people's problems?

Offer solutions to people's challenges?

Exchange value with other people?

Deliver value to other people?

Simone's Story

I introduced Simone in the section on decision-making and problem-solving transparency. Here's Simone's story on finding her calling from a personal perspective:

"Throughout my life, I have always had a deep fascination with how the human brain works. Coupled with my desire to make a positive impact on people, it was only natural that I went into the field of Neuroscience, in particular studying specific receptors in the brains of people diagnosed with Schizophrenia and Bipolar Disorder.

What a super-extraordinary gig that I had, to work in the only Brain Tissue Bank in the Southern Hemisphere, on cutting-edge research, presenting my findings nationally and internationally and to have the impact on potentially millions of people world-wide. I had everything that I desired in my work, but I found that I wasn't happy.

Two years into my work as a post-doctorate, I left the field, never to return. I left my thirst for understanding the machinations of the brain, science experiments and helping people. Through several career shifts, I found myself called into the work of Strategy at a community level and have loved it.

Facilitating the creation of values for an organisation and a vision for the region and seeing these come to life in everyday life, in everyday vocabulary has given me great joy.

It has been through these experiences that I have come to understand a very important desire within myself. Work must have a gratifying element.

You see, the time required within a role in research to see your work come to fruition from bench to bedside is often twenty+ years.

The work that I now do at a closer level to everyday people and the impacts that I see at a regional level in the activities people pursue, vocabulary and also the way the region is portrayed in the media, gives me that sense of gratification that I was missing in my research work.

I often say, that in science, my work was to light up post-mortem human brain tissue using scientific techniques, now I try to light up peoples desires and motivations to dream of a better world and pursue that. This is Heart-Leadership.

Twenty-five ways to move from performance management to Performance Energetics (order not relevant)

1. Stop seeing people as they are. See people as they can be.
2. Find out what's really important to your people and help them achieve it.
3. Assess performance not people.
4. Stop trying to manage people. Instead lead people.
5. Help each employee to create their own personal piece of your strategy execution map.
6. When you assess performance support assessment with data.

7. Provide "feedforward" before feedback and only feedback to people who have asked for it.
8. Focus on standards instead of goals.
9. Discover a shared-view with your employees about where you are, where you're going, why you're going there, how you will get there, who will do what and when, how you will keep progress visible, and how you will behave along the way (culture and values).
10. Teach people to take responsibility for their intentions, feelings, thoughts and actions and then let them be, aside from ongoing helpful conversations.
11. Appreciate people when they do well.
12. Never confuse a person with their performance.
13. Name the elephants in your rooms.
14. Role model candid and authentic conversations.
15. Never review performance and salary at the same time.
16. See problems as opportunities to innovate i.e. change what's normal rather than solve the problem and reinstate the status quo (normal).
17. Keep your promises.
18. Praise in public and only ever offer critique in private, and only then when you been asked or there is an agreement in place for such conversations.
19. Share success stories other people can see and feel themselves in.
20. Be a disruptive influence for good.
21. Be fully present in the now.
22. Only have performance conversations about previously agreed actions. Only change actions with agreement.
23. Focus on processes not outcomes, yet assess performance on outcomes.
24. Do your life's work (see previous) and inspire your employees to

do theirs.

25. Be remarkable at all three pillars of Heart-Leadership: See the checklist below.

Heart-Leadership Pulse Check and Check-up

This is my simplest yet arguably most profound checklist. I complete it with you as part of conducting your Heart-Leadership Check-up.

Heart-Leadership Pulse Check and Check-up please place an ✘ where you are now and a ✓ where you believe you need to move to			
	Good basic standards of performance are being achieved	**Great** above average better than basic	**Remarkable** 'Conspicuously extraordinary'
Hear your Heart (People Leadership) is the art of seeing, sometimes unearthing, mostly magnifying and enhancing people's essence including your own.			
Ask your Head (Process Innovation) is the collaborative work of ensuring processes make it simple for people to bring their essence to their work.			
Engage your Hands (Progress Sustainability) is the joyful craft of ensuring progress towards possibility (desired new reality, shared goal/objective/ aim) is kept visible.			

Turning Possibility Into Reality - further suggested actions

- Conduct an audit of all the conversations you have. Which ones are helpful to other people? Which ones are not? What can you change, modify or nuance to ensure that your conversations are more helpful?

- Over time review transactions and interactions in your organisation /professional practice and positive and negative customer/client feedback/input, and create/update checklists in all areas where you can be more effective and efficient and make it simpler for people to bring their best to their work.

- Invest time and energy in helping all of the people you work closely with to complete their own Career and Life-Calling Card.

Do Your Work.

Notes

1. https://gregmckeown.com/book/

2. https://www.ianberry.biz/courses-and-resources/

3. https://medium.com/@NielsPflaeging/org-physics-the-3-faces-of-every-company-df16025f65f8

4. https://en.wikipedia.org/wiki/Sensemaking

5. We have referenced shared-view previously and will do further. Here's the learning and development link http://www.ianberry.biz/sustaining-shared-view/

6. https://www.amazon.com.au/Checklist-Manifesto-How-Things-Right/dp/0312430000

7. https://future-manifesto.com/index.html

8. Finding Joe https://youtu.be/s8nFACrLxr0

9. Sadly Ken Robinson passed away on the 21st August 2020. He will be greatly missed.

Sparkenation Four

Engage Your Hands and Those of Other People (Progress Sustainability)

*"No one of us has got it all together.
Yet all of us together got it all."*

Scott Wesley-Brown

Overview

Progress sustainability is the joyful craft of ensuring progress towards possibility (desired new reality, shared goal/objective/aim) is kept visible.

In this Sparkenation we're exploring:

- Why reasons, relationships, routines and principles must guide all our actions.

- How our daily conversations with ourselves and our possibility partners and possibility peers keep us focused.

- How the Progress Principle, pre-action rituals and post-action essentials enable us to have a warm heart, a cool head, and a flow in our work through our hands.

Routines and Principles

"There is nothing noble in being superior to your fellow man; true nobility is being superior to your former self."

Ernest Hemingway

Compete with yourself, collaborate with everyone else

In times of uncertainty or crisis, fear often emerges and some people revert to the old command and control behaviour, or take action that is only in their own best interests.

The rush on toilet paper and then other products DC (during coronavirus) is a perfect example of fear and self-interest driven behaviour.

I encourage you to lean in to yourself. Compete with yourself. Seek to collaborate with everyone else.

My online course 'Relationships, Reasons and Routines Guarantee Results'[1] may help you. The course consists of five videos (total viewing time 46 minutes and 38 seconds) and a short workbook.

Following are some of the inspirations, insights, ideas and actions from this course.

- You're accountable for your intentions, feelings, thoughts, and behaviours and actions.
- You're not accountable for anyone else's.
- What other people do or don't do is none of your business. This is sometimes difficult to grasp and accept. Doing so is essential to being the best version of you as well as engaging your hands in flow.

We are all doing our best. One of my all time favourite conversations about this concept is between Russell Brand and Brene Brown[2]. I highly recommend listening to the whole conversation.

Take this 'compete with yourself action' often. You can apply it to any area of your life.

1. Describe an outcome/circumstance you want to improve in your life/work.

2. Then list how you can change/modify/nuance your behaviour, your thoughts, your feelings, your intentions, in relation to what you want to improve. These are the key processes that lead to a change of outcome or circumstance.

Take this 'collaborate with everyone else' action. You can apply it to any relationship in your life.

1. Detail a relationship you want to improve in your life/work.
2. Then list how you can change/modify/nuance your commitment, your finding common ground, how you make connection, the regularity and kind of contact you have with the person you want to improve your relationship with. These are the key processes that lead to an improved relationship.

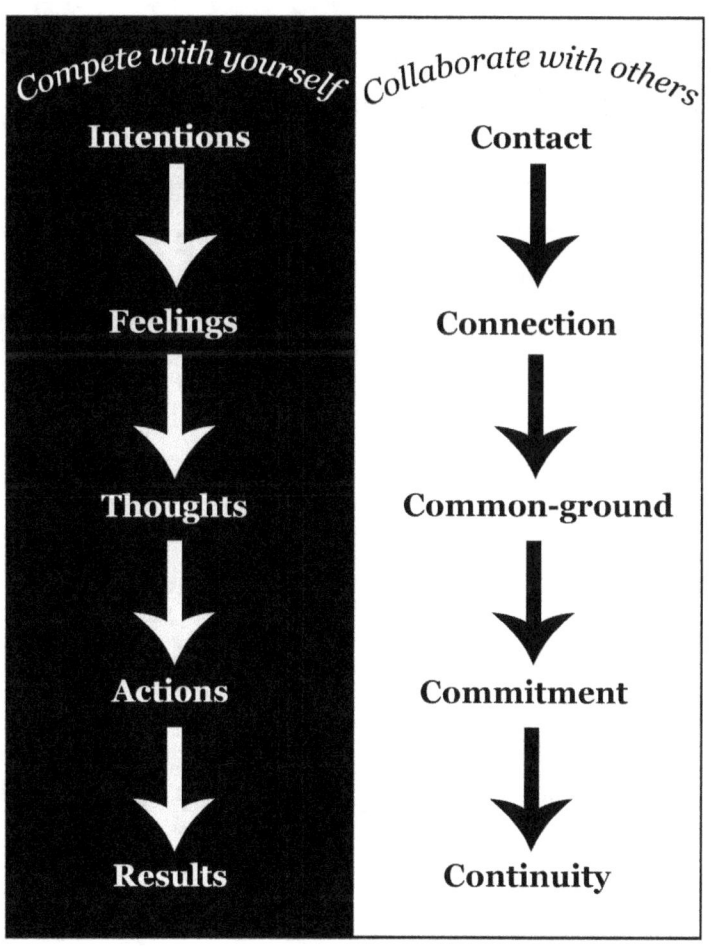

What's worth celebrating in your life and work? and What can be better?

I've been asking myself these two questions every day for more than forty years.

I believe they are two very powerful questions because they ensure I begin every day grateful and focused.

Try the above yourself for at least a month. It will help you to ensure that this year is your best year yet. Maybe this will become a life-long habit!

For more than a quarter of a century these two questions have been the foundational Performance Energetic conversations used by my clients. Several clients begin their team meetings with answers to these questions.

These two questions are critical in the quest of competing with yourself and collaborating with everyone else.

Quantum Leaps
and the aggregation of marginal gains

The best way that I know of to achieve everything of value is one small yet significant step at a time.

Now is the only moment that matters.

Some people live in the past. Their focus is on what happened.

Some people are future focused. Their focus is on what might happen.

The most successful and happy people are crystal clear on where they're going and their focus is on what will happen in the present.

Now Over Normal

Brad Smith is the COO of Gallagher Bassett in Australia. Brad is a resident of my Heart-Leadership Online Village. He is a kindred spirit.

Brad shared the following with me.

"During a period of Covid lockdown I organised a virtual coffee catch up with 30 or so of my Victorian front line leadership.

One of our senior managers, asked if I could provide any tips on how I balance home and work life in our largely virtual world. Naturally I provided a response, suggesting that rhythm and routine seemed to work best for me, ensuring I'm up early enough to be ready for work, shedding the initial baggy pants and t-shirt regime and making sure I respect the times that are in my diary. It takes a ruthless discipline of course and I'll be honest in saying that I should at times practice what I preach.

I had a light bulb moment when I realised we need to keep talking about these things, sharing experiences to support one another, and providing learning examples which just might be relevant.

There is no singular solution and in many ways our people need to "tailor" what works best for them to navigate the now.

Out of our coffee catch-ups we developed a mantra 'accept the now/ appreciate the now', which has been a catalyst in embracing now over normal.

The wonderful phrase "Now over Normal" was the title in a communique from our President and CEO. A phrase worthy of consideration for both now and in days to come."

Two of my great realisations about thriving on the challenges of change came about as a consequence of being involved in a rapidly failing change program. I learned:

- Change cannot be managed, manoeuvred, or manipulated.
- Change is a process not a program.

I like John Kotter's famous 'eight steps for leading change' model[3] however I feel it is often too complicated or that not every step is needed.

Over time I co-created the change process pictured through work with my clients.

I am also very grateful to the work of David Cooperrider whose Appreciative Inquiry[4] process has greatly inspired and influenced my work.

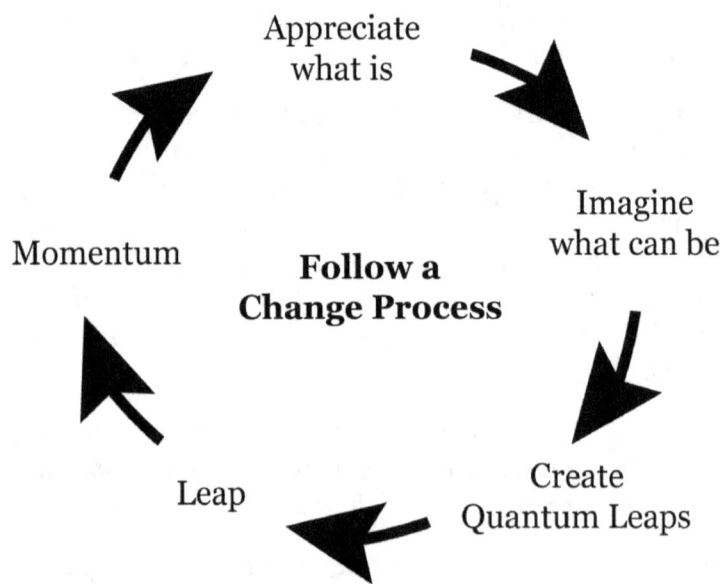

Appreciating What Is

I have taken many people through the following five questions in order to zero in on reality in any chosen area. In less than an hour great insights can be gleaned:

1. What's remarkable? i.e. conspicuously extraordinary?
2. What's great? i.e. above average; better than basic?
3. What's good? i.e. basic standards of performance are being achieved?
4. What's bad? i.e. of poor quality or low standard?
5. What's ugly? i.e. unpleasant, displeasing, or threatening personal or business well-being?

Imagining what can be

I have found that the simplest way to shift from reality to possibility is to choose one area at a time from answers to the 'appreciating what is' questions and then.

1. Describe in a present tense sentence what the new reality feels and looks like.
2. Decide who you are going to engage to work with you to ensure the shift happens. Then move to creating quantum leaps with them.

Create Quantum Leaps

The common view of a quantum leap is that it is a big jump. In actual fact a quantum leap is a very small change. The significance is that it's a direct jump from here to there. I call them small yet significant shifts. We will look at some actual quantum leaps in the next section on Plans and Alternatives.

Leap

Actually take action. A lot of people have good intentions, even detailed plans, and then don't do the work.

This is one reason I say the words *"Do Your Work"* so often!

Momentum

The best way that I have discovered to gain and sustain momentum is the aggregation of marginal gains which is the philosophy of searching for a tiny margin of improvement in everything you do.

I first learned about this philosophy from this article by James Clear[5]

This from the article

"Most people love to talk about success (and life in general) as an event. We talk about losing 50 pounds or building a successful business or winning the Tour de France as if they are events. But the truth is that most of the significant things in life aren't stand-alone events, but rather the sum of all the moments when we chose to do things one percent better or one percent worse. Aggregating these marginal gains makes a difference."

Reviewing your leaps via an after-action-review is a great way to aggregate.

To recap - an after-action-review answers the following questions

- What happened and why?
- What did you learn, relearn, and unlearn (or let go of)?
- How can you be better, wiser and more valuable in applying your learnings?
- Who will we become?
- What will we do next?

Invoke key actions of your hands

The following actions are crucial to engaging your hands and those of other people.

Expressive

When I made the decision to ensure that every action I take is an expression of my DNA and leaves a unique mark like my fingerprint or signature, I became much more considered about my actions.

Such expressiveness is a foundation stone of Heart-Leadership.

Patience

Being patient is not natural for me. Applying the science of quantum leaps, i.e. small yet significant shifts, has helped me to enhance the skill over time.

In addition as I pay greater attention to my natural heart rhythm which I have referenced is slow, I get better still. These nuances have helped me to better my sense-making in my head and be patient for the results to come naturally after I take action.

Such patience is a foundation stone of Heart-Leadership.

Quality

Taking less actions, indeed doing less work, means quality has come to the fore. It's an old adage yet I find it to be true that focusing on taking quality actions is better than quantity.

Such quality is a foundation stone of Heart-Leadership.

Reliability

A focus on quality of course helps us in being reliable. I'm finding more and more that reliability within itself is a key to exchanging and delivering value. Of course our reliability is a key component of being trustworthy. In a decidedly digital world trust is what makes us decisively human.

Such reliability is a foundation stone of Heart-Leadership.

Flow

Being in the zone is the place all athletes and professional practitioners desire. For us Heart-Leaders flow is a consequence of hearing our hearts first, then thinking things through via the head-catalysts, which act as a springboard for hand actions.

Such flow is a foundation stone of Heart-Leadership.

Flexibility

For many years now flexibility has been in the top echelon of what employees want from employers. Being flexible, I believe, is one way to stay in harmony with ourselves and other people as we do work we love in the service of people who love what we do.

Such flexibility is a foundation stone of Heart-Leadership.

Value delivery

The key measure of any output is determining whether or not the result was as valuable as we promised or agreed it would be. Value is in the eyes of the beholder.

Such value delivery is a foundation stone of Heart-Leadership.

Innovation

To have successfully shifted away from the status quo ,when sameness was no longer serving, is innovation. As we have explored every day innovation is desirable and imminently possible.

Such innovation is a foundation stone of Heart-Leadership.

The following is the flow of each of these eight hand actions from the eight heart qualities and the eight head catalysts.

Heart Qualities	Head Catalysts	Hand Actions
Love	Openness	Expressive
Gratitude	Sense-making	Patience
Appreciation	Decision-making	Quality
Care	Problem-solving	Reliability
Happiness	Imagination	Flow
Compassion	Human centred design	Flexibility
Harmony	Systems thinking	Value delivery
Kindness	Curiosity	Innovation

The following story from Rosemary McKenzie-Ferguson, the Founder of Craig's Table illustrates brilliantly much of the flow of the above.

"I have always believed in heart based leadership.

Craig's Table had only been opened a short time, my role had me going to meetings and networking away from the location so it was fair to say many of the participants really had no idea as to who I was or what I was meant to be doing.

One particular day I was meant to be catching up on the dreaded paperwork so I was going to work from my unit instead of the office where I was constantly interrupted.

Engage Your Hands 117

However as things turned out I was called to the office, so I went dressed in my jeans and top, I did what had to be done, and then proceeded to help with the end of day tidy up which involved taking some things up to Bay One (our version of the Men's Shed).

Whilst I was putting things away one of the participants asked me if I could help him tidy up and as he was running a bit late would I sweep the floor.

So I swept the floor and we chatted all the while it took about fifteen minutes to get things set right in order to shut the shed for the night.

The participant left and I finished doing a few things to give myself a head start for the next day.

About two weeks went past I had totally forgotten about sweeping the shed floor. I hadn't forgotten the conversation which to me was the main thing.

I pulled into the car park and got out of the car dressed in the semi-corporate clothing that I normally wear.

The participant who asked me to sweep the floor came running over to see me. He got my briefcase out of the boot and then just stood there I asked if there was something wrong, he said he needed to apologise to me for his asking me to sweep the floor, he didn't know that I was the Founder and that he hoped I would forgive him for the disrespect I must have felt.

It was clear that he was quite upset for the slight he assumed I would be feeling.

So I asked him a simple question "Did the floor need to be swept?' he answered yes, I followed "Did you ask me if I had time to do the task?" he answered yes, I asked did we have a great chat and did he get away on time to pick his children up from school?" he answered yes.

I then said at Craig's Table there is no hierarchy, if a tasks needs to be done then whoever is free at the time can do the task, if that is me then that is me no questions no qualms as long as everyone is happy that is the only requirement.

This man went on to buy his own small business. The last time I saw him he told me that he had learnt more about business management and how to respect staff through this experience than anywhere else. His great learning was understanding the vast difference between operating as an hierarchy and leading from the heart."

Plans and Alternatives

"Success is a few simple disciplines, practiced every day; while failure is simply a few errors in judgment, repeated every day."

Jim Rohn

Performance Possibility Plans-on-a-page

I'm one of the pioneers of Plan's-on-a-page. I swear by them as one of the most magnificent tools there is to help us to take action and achieve what's important to us.

I first created a plan-on-a-page in my notebook with a trusted direct report in August 1989. I called it a Performance Possibility plan-on-a-page.

I had twenty-four direct reports at the time in multiple locations and thousands of miles apart! My deep desire was to find a way to keep everyone on the same page collectively and in individual locations.

People started calling them PPP's and this label is still used by many of my clients today!

Plans-on-a-page or PPP's are a remarkable way to

1. Keep focused personally, for a team, for an organisation.
2. Help you and others (particularly those people to whom you have promised to deliver value) to be accountable.
3. Sustain a shared-view with your performance possibility partners (colleagues, mentors) and possibility peers in areas you have agreed are significant. More on partners and peers in the Conversation piece of this Sparkenation.
4. Own your piece of the execution quilt or jigsaw.
5. Capture in one place the quantum leaps (small yet significant shifts) you're taking to move from current reality to possibility (your next reality).

Following are some versions of my current plan-on-a-page. First an explanation on number 4. above.

One of my most prized possessions is a small quilt my Nana Ruby Sherriff made over 50 years ago. I have wonderful memories of her and Pa Fred. They lived less than a mile from me when I was a boy, so I was a frequent visitor to their house.

A vivid memory is Nana making quilts. There'd be a pieces here and others over there and then one day it would all magically come together. It would be one quilt and yet each individual piece stood out.

Little did I know then that Nana's quilts would many years later inspire a remarkable idea.

In business strategy is like a compass and execution a map. For your strategy to be executed every employee needs their unique piece of the map. I call it a quilt map. Performance Possibility Plans (PPPs) are an individuals piece of the quilt.

Visual plans-on-a-page work best

Over time my plans-on-a-page have become more visual, as have those of people who have worked with the concept for awhile.

My current personal PPP as at September 2020 is pictured as an example:

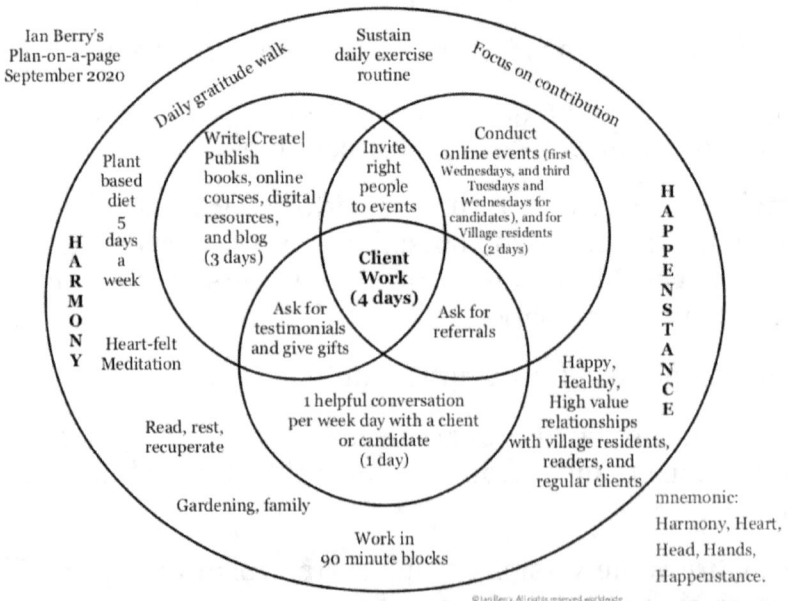

Although I prefer more visually appealing PPP's I still often create them initially like below.

This example uses the seven areas of significance in shared-view[6] as a guide to creation.

Plan and Co-Promises on a page Ian Berry.
Performance Period: 1/4/20 - 31/7/20

Reality	Possibility
Have 3 retainer clients.	Have 6 -12 clients at any given time with 6 on retainer.

Purpose	Strategy
Inspire and support my clients to see and bring out the best in people, including themselves. In harmony with business process improvements and sustainable progress, in order to achieve their best results at the least personal and business costs.	Attract new clients primarily through getting referrals via centres of influence and colleagues to online and in person events and then converting a percentage in follow-through + 'stay in touch' conversations with candidates. .

Key quantum leaps are:
1. Give value in advance without attachment to getting back through.
2. Magnificence in publishing (blog, podcast, videos, ebooks, books, tools, tips, templates and techniques) and sharing these complimentary.
3. One-of-a-kind online and in-person events.
4. Direct contact and innovative connection with existing relationships.

Progress	Culture
Key Human Indicators are:	• Daily Meditation and Gratitude.
1. continuing to automatically receive requests to do work from people who love my work. 2. continuing to receive referrals without asking for them. 3. continuing to receive requests for extensions.	• Continuous Noticing and Contributing and Sustaining and Enhancing relationships. • All of above without attachment to outcomes. • Feeling valued, fulfilled and loved and helping others to feel the same. • Everthing always works out for me/us mantra.

The rhythm needed to sustain action comes from our regular rituals

An alternative to plans-on-a-page like the ones above is to focus on capturing your rituals on a page.

One of my long standing versions of performance possibility plans-on-a-page has been the rituals documented below.

I know from experience that if I follow the right processes for me then the outcomes take care of themselves.

Here are my most recent personal and professional rituals.

Personal Rituals

Daily

Write down who and what I'm grateful for or say out loud while walking.

Maintain "attitude of gratitude".

Heart-focused meditation.

Exercise - take a brisk 30 minute walk AM and undertake exercise regime PM.

Family time - ensure such is a priority.

Relaxation - take time out to relax after working in 90 minute focused bursts. Just sit and think or just sit time - without smart phone.

Write 500 words minimum.

Eat a healthy diet based primarily on vegetables and fruit five days a week. Fast regularly.

Weekly

Work in the garden or around home, or do some different physical activity. Turn my phone off while doing so.

Enjoy at least one family member and/or friend activity.

Others

12 weeks holiday as "mini-retirements", scheduled in advance.

Visit in person with children and grandchildren at least twice per year.

> **Professional Rituals (working 25 hours per week maximum)**
>
> Write every day.
>
> **Sunday or before:** write blog post for Monday.
>
> **Monday:**
>
> 11 am Heart Leadership Village conversation;
>
> One HC (helpful conversation with a client, colleague or candidate);
>
> Up to 90 minutes PM session with a Client;
>
> Social media share and spread.
>
> **Tuesday:**
>
> Write and record Wednesday video and write accompanying blog post;
>
> One HC;
>
> PM client session (two clients if more than one event scheduled for Wednesday).
>
> **Wednesday:**
>
> 3.30 PM event on first Wednesday (NZ, Australia, ASIA, UAE).
>
> Other Wednesdays this time plus 10 AM (NZ, Australia, USA) and 6 PM for (UK/Europe);
>
> One HC;
>
> Client session if only one event.
>
> Social media share and spread.
>
> **Thursday:**
>
> Write and record Friday podcast and write accompanying blog post;
>
> One HC:
>
> One Client session.
>
> **Friday:**
>
> One HC.
>
> Social media share and spread.

My favourite insight into rituals comes from the 19th century humourist Josh Billings who said *"Consider the postage stamp: its usefulness consists in the ability of sticking to one thing until it gets done."*

Of course postage stamps may very soon be a relic of the past, nevertheless the principle of sticking to one thing until it gets done is timeless.

Health challenges have meant having to change my lifestyle and work habits in order to maximise my energy levels.

I have reduced my working hours by about a quarter a month. I now work around 100 hours a month. Not surprisingly to me I have not lost any productivity, I am doing my best work, and I am providing better value to my clients. This is possible because the rituals I follow enable me to maintain my rhythm.

My heart beat is slow. It's been this way since birth. I do my best work when I am slow and considered. This doesn't mean that I cannot act fast when needed, rather it means that flow happens when I am slow and considered.

Recently I had to have an ultra-sound of my heart done to check on possible side affects from the drugs I have to take to keep my melanoma at bay. It was incredible to watch my own heart beating and the experience gave me a great reminder of my natural rhythm.

What is the pace of your heart beat?

Here's how I have changed my rituals to match my circumstances.

I apply the Rule of Three. I'm sure you're familiar with many famous three's. The theory is we can easily remember three. And it works in practice.

The 'Rule of Three' is pervasive everywhere in our society. Think stories, fairy tales and myths, and the lines from history that inspire us

"Friends, Romans, Countrymen."

"Blood, sweat and tears."

"The good, the bad and the ugly."

Personal

In my case personally my BIG three are heart-focused meditation, diet and exercise. I picture them simply like this:

Personal Daily Rituals

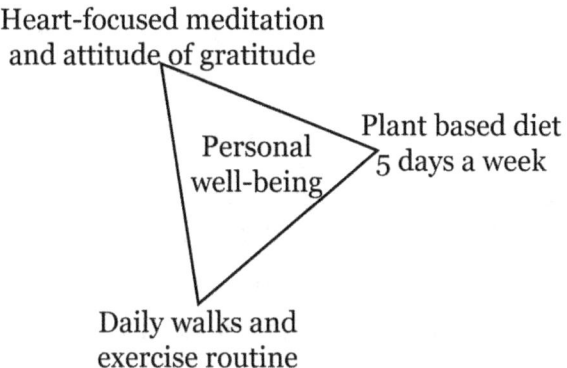

Professional

In my professional practice my BIG three are books, courses and resources, events and helpful conversations. I picture them simply like this:

My Work
(10 days a month, 10 months of the year)

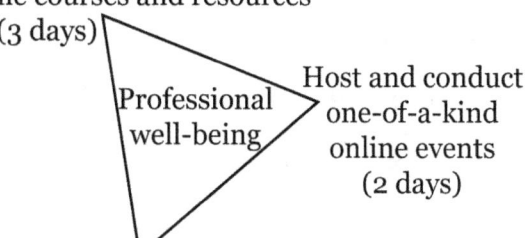

Do you live and work in alignment with your rhythm?

Are there nuances you are still to make to ensure better flow in your life?

What are your life and work rituals?

How could you capture them visually to help you to maintain focus and flow?

Beware of the barriers of busyness

"How's thing's going?" I ask my client as we sit down for our scheduled catch-up. *"I'm as busy as I've ever been in my life"*, is his reply. *"Busy doing what?"* I ask.

Our conversation gets interesting because upon close inspection we find being busy doesn't necessarily mean productive or valuable!

I am often reminded of the barriers of busyness. I meet a lot of people bound up by busyness.

Here are the fifteen common tell tale signs:

1. Decision-making processes not being followed.
2. Problems are solved and then they re-occur over and over again. This has a lot to do with problem-solving being mostly about reinstating the status quo rather than changing what's normal (innovation).
3. Decisions being continually revisited.
4. Documentation is produced in lieu of action.
5. Meetings occur with key players absent.
6. Meetings have no agendas.
7. Meetings are poorly conducted.
8. Whiteboards full.
9. Diaries full.
10. Inboxes full.
11. There's a pre-occupation with mobile phones and other devices. If you can't have mobile free days without withdrawal symptoms

you're in the grip of "time famine".

12. Negative body language of staff.

13. Management (PPPPS's - policies, procedures, practices, processes, philosophies, structures and systems) mean it isn't simple for people to bring their best to their work every day.

14. Leaders who love the sound of their own voice and the corresponding lack of awareness means they are oblivious to the chaos and complication that they are causing.

15. Massive confusion exists between what is communication and what is information sharing.

Here are ten tips to ensure that you are not bound by busyness:

1. Educate yourself and others that communication requires sending, receiving and that it results in agreement even if it is agreeing to disagree. Information sharing on the other hand is one way.

2. Refuse to attend meetings where there is no agenda available well in advance. Don't discuss anything not on the agenda when you're in the actual meeting.

3. Review your efficiency and effectiveness weekly, monthly, fortnightly, quarterly, and yearly. A great way to be disciplined is to create and follow a rituals document like we have explored above.

4. Set aside time each week to do nothing. I sit under a tree somewhere for several hours per week. It is amazing how refreshed we can feel just by doing nothing.

5. Get your leadership (people) and management (process) harmony right for you. For some of us it is 80% leadership and 20% management, for others it's the other way round. There are many other possible combinations. Remember leadership is about people and effectiveness. Management is about processes and efficiency. Leadership is art, management a practice. The two must be in harmony for us to be the best we can be.

6. Do not tolerate negativity in any shape or form.

7. Block out a lot of space in your diary and/or rituals document

where nothing is planned. You will be astounded at how much more effective you become when your diary is no longer full.

8. Work on things that are important and urgent. Forget the rest.

9. Celebrate process more than outcome.

10. Spend time with positive children as often as possible. They have an amazing sense of self, initiative, curiosity, creativity and wonder.

Turning Possibility Into Reality - further suggested actions

My recommended actions to get started on creating your possibility plan-on-a-page are:

1. Take an A4 page and write 7 headings i.e. reality, possibility, purpose, strategy, execution, progress, and culture.

2. Under Reality write 1 - 3 paragraphs about your current status in your chosen key performance areas.

3. Under Possibility write 1 - 3 paragraphs about your goals for this performance period i.e. the next 90 days, in those same key performance areas.

4. Under Purpose write 1 paragraph about your reason for being.

5. Under Strategy write one sentence about how you will move from reality to possibility.

6. Under Execution write 1 - 3 paragraphs about your key tactics to execute your strategy.

7. Under Progress write 1 - 3 paragraphs about how you will make progress in meaningful work visible and how you will communicate, and converse about progress towards possibility.

8. Under Culture write 1 - 3 paragraphs about how you will further inspire and influence people to be accountable for living the agreed behaviours.

9. Share what you have written with your team mates and colleagues and make adjustments.

There you have it. You now have your first PPP!

Now create a visual of your PPP.

Do Your Work.

Candid, convivial, compassionate, conscious, and compelling conversations

The greatest conversations have these five components.

The noun 'conversation' comes from the Old French word of the same spelling, meaning *"manner of conducting oneself in the world."* You'll find that keeping this in mind is a great habit to sustain in your mastery of conversations.

I have long maintained that there are eight conversations that count.

Here is an overview of each:

Self-talk is the most important. Self-talk is the continual conversation you have with yourself that overcomes your 'resistance' and engages the very best version of you. We'll return to Self-talk shortly.

Peer review is the daily conversations you have with your peers that appreciate remarkable work and help everyone to be seeing, unearthing, magnifying and enhancing their essence and the essence of others. Having focusing tools is paramount such as Performance Possibility Plans on-a-page or Rituals on-a-page, Role Clarity Statements and Career and Life-calling Cards. We'll return to peer conversations shortly when we explore Possibility Peers.

Feedforward is suggestions from others that provide insight and foresight for you to change your behaviour. These are far more powerful than feedback. For more on Feedforward please re-read Sparkenation 9 in my Changing What's Normal[7] book and/or google Feedforward and Marshall Goldsmith.

Feedback is gifts of hindsight from others about the past to assist you in learning from actions taken or not. I regard feedback as the least valuable of these eight and only personally listen to feedback from people I trust and whom I have asked.

After-action-reviews I have already referenced several times.

After-action-reviews are structured conversations that appreciate what was remarkable, great, good, bad, and ugly about a specific action; imagine what can be next time; create/update PPPs/Ritual on-a-page in ways that reflect agreed personal and professional behaviour changes, and keep, cease, begin actions.

After-action- reviews are also essential for determining how you will integrate new learnings and perceptions with what is already working well for you.

Weekly Check-ins are short, sharp, weekly meetings online and/or in person where individuals and/or teams review what's happened and what's next, and agree on actions and accountability for the coming week.

Mentor Moments are essential for Heart-Leaders because we each need someone to lean on, trust, and share with, who are outside our usual environments yet understanding of them.

Good mentors are willing to:

- Influence others regarding the steps necessary to lift performance yet allow others to make their own decisions.
- Listen more than speak.
- Give advice when asked but more to encourage people to find their own way.
- Experience delayed gratification.
- Freely share hard earned wisdom.

COO Coffee Connect

My client, and a member of the Heart-Leadership Online Village, Brad Smith is the COO of Gallagher Basset. Brad has a virtual coffee with his employees he calls 'COO Coffee Connect'. Here's part of an email Brad sent to his employees. It reflects the spirit of Check-ins and Mentor Moments.

"Firstly the sessions are completely voluntary. If you choose to book some time with me, you may use that time however you think best. It may be for some mentoring type discussions (or indeed mentoring me), maybe a think tank, a Q&A session, anything that you feel would benefit you in your current role or career aspirations.

The only thing I ask is that you come to the session prepared with what you'd like to discuss with me, or what you'd like to get from the session.

The onus will be on you to make our time together work for you.

Rest assured there's something in it for me also, and that is, to keep the open dialogue between all of us alive and well."

The majority of successful people I know are part of one or more mastermind groups (people mutually committed to each others' success who meet regularly). We'll return to master-mind groups shortly when we explore Possibility Peers and Possibility Partners. As you will see I now call these groups Heart-Leadership Peer Groups.

Being candid, convivial, compassionate, conscious, and compelling starts with self-talk.

Being decisively human in a decidedly digital world means overcoming the deterioration of great conversation and communication that is evident in many organisations.

Deterioration has occurred, I believe, because there's absence in the online world of these five energisers that bring alive heart qualities.

Instead we're confronted by fake news, deliberate distribution of disinformation, and dehumanising behaviour where the culprits are often world leaders.

Add to these a social media landscape where being anti-social and 'full of rage' is rampant, and you begin to see why a new kind of conversation is both desired and needed.

Candid

Candour is critical to the culture of Pixar and Walt Disney Animation Studios and a key reason for their long term success.

And it can be at your place too. I recommend the book 'Creativity Inc.' by the co-founder of Pixar, Ed Catmull[8], for deep insights into cultures of candour.

Convivial

Some people struggle with the bluntness of candour and so I find conviviality helps. Some synonyms for convivial: friendly, genial, affable, amiable, congenial, agreeable, good-humoured, cordial, warm, sociable, outgoing, gregarious. We're all capable of these character traits when we're being the best version of ourselves and leading with heart.

Compassionate

We have already established that compassion is a heart quality and a foundation stone of Heart-Leadership.

The following from the Dalai Lama XIV[9] says it all for me:

"We can reject everything else: religion, ideology, all received wisdom. But we cannot escape the necessity of love and compassion.... This, then, is my true religion, my simple faith.

In this sense, there is no need for temple or church, for mosque or synagogue, no need for complicated philosophy, doctrine or dogma. Our own heart, our own mind, is the temple. The doctrine is compassion. Love for others and respect for their rights and dignity, no matter who or what they are: ultimately these are all we need.

So long as we practice these in our daily lives, then no matter if we are learned or unlearned, whether we believe in Buddha or God, or follow some other religion or none at all, as long as we have compassion for others and conduct ourselves with restraint out of a sense of responsibility, there is no doubt we will be happy."

Conscious

We are living in a time of a choice between a consciousness revolution and the so-called Fourth Industrial Revolution portrayed by the World Economic Forum.

I believe that we are still recovering from the nasty hangover from the first industrial revolution where it was assumed we could treat people like machines. Each industrial revolution since has been allowed to further dehumanise us.

For sure, disruptive technologies and the Internet of Things (IoT), robotics, virtual reality (VR) and artificial intelligence (AI) etc., etc., the so-called Fourth Industrial Revolution, are changing the way we live and work. My question is *"are they changing things for a better human experience?"* I am extremely skeptical that they are.

There's even talk of a fifth industrial revolution where technology and humans converge. This does not resonate with my heart.

I want to be a better human and so my focus is on increasing my levels of self-awareness and my awareness of others, the number one and two skills of leadership. I'm only interested in technology when it enhances these skills.

Compelling

I wrote a paper recently with my friend and colleague Gary Edwards about this[10]. In the paper we say:

"In some way every conversation we have every day is about change.

Some believe that change can be managed and that we can persuade people to change.

We say change cannot be managed. We believe change is a process.

People are beyond being persuaded to change. Persuasion means that they don't really want to change, but feel as though they have no choice.

Instead, people are looking for a compelling reason to change - a vision and a process that they can embrace and get behind with enthusiasm.

When an argument for change is persuasive, the person can say Yes - but might only do so because they believe they have to. Yet when an argument for change is compelling, they can't say No - and they don't want to."

Being candid, convivial, compassionate, conscious, and compelling are not only fundamental to every conversation you have with yourself, they are also fundamental to every conversation you have with other people.

Here are the others as a reminder:

- Safe, peer group environment,
- High energy,
- Humour,
- Prominence given to curiosity, sense of wonder and generosity,

- Heart stirring and thought shifting moments,
- Relevant, timely, immediately useable content that is also highly valuable in the long term,
- Leads you to small yet significant shifts (quantum leaps) you decide to make in your own best way.

In every conversation that I host online and in person the quest is to enable and inspire all of the above.

My long term client and friend, Jamie Wilson, Victorian Regional Sales Manager Haymes Paint shared the following with me. It is a great story of candid, convivial, compassionate, conscious, and compelling conversation and being a Performance Possibility which we explore next.

"After a recent "Heart Leadership" session, I immediately contacted a work college and close friend to have a conversation with him regarding some personal issues he was having in his life that he had shared with me a week earlier.

The issues were that he and his wife were fighting a lot and were drifting apart, not communicating or spending any quality time together and were letting their heads control their conversations and feelings and were not letting their hearts do the talking.

As the session was progressing, I took my notes in relation to the context they delivered but then related them to his situation and gave him a call.

I presented my notes and thoughts to him, as I deeply care for both he, his wife and his children. What I spoke to him about and suggested were some questions and thoughts:

Starting with feelings from your heart

1. *Why did we get together in the 1st place?*
2. *What happened in our relationship to get to this point? Be honest and talk from the heart with real feelings. Have facts not hearsays.*
3. *Work though what's possible in our relationship moving forward if we can both agree to the outcomes we want and can achieve?*

4. Ensure this is exactly what you both want.

5. Lay out a clear plan and path of how you are going to get there together.

6. Ask what I can do to help us get there.

7. And lastly, "is there anything else"

After some tears and emotional conversation between he and I, he agreed these thoughts were exactly what he needed to drive the conversations and outcomes moving forward with his wife and I can happily say that months down the track, they are both in a far better place and working hard to ensure their marriage is as happy and fruitful as when they tied the knot 13 years earlier.

These conversations are also vital when engaging and communicating with your staff when things aren't quite going as you planned or agreed to.

The learning for me through this exercise has been to always go back to the purpose and reason as the starting point to any conversation when having to deal with difficult situations. Leading from the heart, talk from the heart and then letting my head and hands drive the outcomes."

The Power of Performance Possibility Partners

Having Performance Possibility Partners is perfect for practicing and enhancing our conversation and communication attitudes and skills.

Performance Possibility Partners are people we trust, who have our best interests at heart, and who are non-judgmental of our performance.

Performance Possibility Partners can be family members, friends, mentors, coaches, advisors, anyone who is not directly involved in our work, yet has expertise to inspire, encourage, and support us.

We all need others to magnify and enhance our essence.

In particular Performance Possibility Partners are people we have chosen to be there for us as we take action and to hold us to account when our performance is less than we have agreed it will be.

The Power of Performance Possibility Peers

Performance Possibility Peers are colleagues in the same organisation as us or they are people who are on a similar path in other organisations.

In either case we form master-mind groups or peer groups (I call mine Heart-Leadership Peer Groups) as a way to share stories and make decisions about how we will change, modify or nuance our performance.

As mentioned previously, during the writing of this book I formed my latest Heart-Leadership Peer Group called The Heart-Leadership Online Village[11].

In the Village we are performance possibility partners and peers for people wanting to be the best Heart-Leaders we can be at home, and in the workplace, town, city, country, sporting club, community group, wherever we belong.

Here is the short version back story:

I've been engaged in master-mind groups for over 30 years. The first was a bunch of blokes who met weekly to explore what it really meant to be great husbands and fathers as well as true friends. We called ourselves 'The JourneyMen' and were referenced by Steve Biddulph in one of his early books on Manhood. There was nothing much happening for men in those days and domestic violence and other matters were just starting to be discussed more openly.

I'm in no doubt that we all became better people because of our regular candid conversations (often around the pot belly stove) in Philip's shed.

Since then I've been a member of many groups, led quite a few, and presented to over 100 around the world in the leadership peer-group space.

The original idea put forward by Napoleon Hill in his famous book 'Think and Grow Rich' still holds true: *"The co-ordination of knowledge and effort of two or more people, who work toward a definitive purpose, in the spirit of harmony...no two minds ever come together without thereby creating a third, invisible intangible force, which may be likened to a third mind"* (the Mastermind).

What has emerged in more recent times is that people want to gather to not just engage with our minds, we want to engage in our hearts too.

We want to do this work with people we trust, who believe in us and appreciate us, yet also challenge us.

We want to belong to places where we can be candid.

We want to share our dreams. Sure we want considered responses to our requests, mostly we want to share what is in our hearts.

Where do you belong?

The most remarkable leaders I know are in the habit of regularly stepping off the field of play to work on themselves and on their organisations.

Because of the wonders of technology, the majesty of Heart-Leadership groups can now happen online where we can tap into the wisdom of peers operating in non-competitive businesses and from different countries and cultures.

I regard having a mentor/s and belonging to a peer group/s as the top two essentials for personal and professional growth.

One of the reasons that I host online conversations every month is because, for the regulars, they are a form of Heart-Leadership peer group.

Of course the concept of a peer groups shifts to a whole new level when we consider them in the light of heart, head and hands and in that order.

There is nothing quite like belonging to groups of peers where the focus is on hearing our hearts first, then asking heads, and then being with one another/working with one another as we engage our hands.

Performance Possibility Peers as with Performance Possibility Partners are special kinds of friends.

Many are called, only a few take the next step into the unknown. We act alone yet we need others to walk alongside us while answering their own call at the same time.

> *"A friend is someone who knows the song in your heart and can sing it back to you when you have forgotten the words."* **Anon**

Turning Possibility Into Reality - further suggested actions

- Establish a deliberate practice to always be working on enhancing your conversation, communication and presentation skills.

- Belong to professional associations and master-mind peer groups that include the above.

- Begin your own master-mind peer group.

- Contact me and ask to be invited to join or to be placed on the waiting list to become a resident in the Heart-Leadership Online Village. We are a small group limited to 24 residents at any one time.

Do Your Work.

Focus

"Always remember, your focus determines your reality."

George Lucas

Your focus as a Heart-Leader is on having a warm heart, a cool head, and a flow in your work through your hands.

There are three keys to this focus, adapting 'The Progress Principle' and what you do before and after you take action.

The Progress Principle

For most of my fifty years working life I've observed that, in the very best workplaces, progress towards shared objectives has been visible via scorecards and/or scoreboards of some kind.

When 'The Balanced Scorecard' concept began to be adopted from 1996 not only did the pictures get better, so did what was being pictured.

In the last decade there's been a further raising of the bar as the wisest people apply 'The Progress Principle' which was rated by Harvard Business Review as the breakthrough idea of 2010. I highly recommend getting the book by Teresa Amabile and Steven Kramer.[12]

The Progress Principle is *"making progress in meaningful work visible."*

I've never thought much of the idea that 'what gets measured gets done'. I'm much more aligned with the following:

"Not everything that counts can be counted, and not everything that can be counted counts."

William Bruce Cameron

in 'Informal Sociology' published 1963.

For Heart-Leaders our meaningful work is primarily work that leads to people feeling valued, living values, and exchanging and delivering agreed value.

This book has shone a light on the three pillars of this work: people leadership, process innovation, and progress sustainability.

Here's a reminder of them:

Hear Your Heart and the hearts of other people (People leadership) is the art of seeing, sometimes unearthing, mostly magnifying and enhancing people's essence including your own.

Ask Your Head and Valuing Greatly The Minds of Others (Process innovation) is the collaborative work of ensuring processes make it simple for people to bring their essence to their work.

Remember processes include policies, procedures, practices, philosophies, principles, structures and systems.

Engage Your Hands and Those of Other People (Progress sustainability) is the joyful craft of ensuring that progress towards possibility (desired new reality, shared goal/objective/aim) is kept visible.

We have already described some tools that keep our progress in meaningful work visible, such as Performance Possibility Plans-on-a-page and Rituals-on-a-page.

There are many more. I see traffic lights, graphs, thermometers and the like everywhere.

What visual formats will you use, that people will engage with, to be "making progress in meaningful work visible"?

Pre-Action Rituals

The function of ritual, as I understand it, is to give form to human life, not in the way of mere surface arrangement, but in depth.

Joseph Campbell

Below are regular actions that I take personally and professionally.

As you review my rituals begin to determine your own and how you can apply the principles herein in your own best way.

Appointments

I'm early for all appointments. I take the time to place my hand on my heart and feel my own unique rhythm.

I then turn my attention to the desires and expectations of the person or people I'm about to meet. I reflect on how everything is possible when we meet each other in our hearts first and then ask our heads and engage our hands.

Blogging

I write a minimum of 500 words every day. It's a ritual I have followed for over 35 years. Some of the words end up in a blog post. I've been blogging since May 2007 and for several years now I post Mondays, Wednesdays and Fridays.

I've learned that regularity and relevance are valued by my subscribers. I've also learned that people value variety and so now Mondays is a read only, Wednesdays a video too, and Fridays a podcast as well as a read. Read, Watch, Listen have become a mantra.

I also keep my videos under 5 minutes and podcasts under 10 minutes. The right people for me don't want anything long-winded.

Helpful Conversations

As referenced earlier, Bernadette Jiwa's concept that marketing is a series of 'helpful conversations' has been a game-changer for me. I have no desire to market or sell in any of the traditional ways. I accept that we must put ourselves out there.

Helpful Conversations are exactly that, helpful. I know that the more helpful I am to the right people for me, the more valuable they perceive my input, then the more naturally people ask for my professional services.

Creating online courses

Short and succinct with specific outcomes in mind is what that right people for me tell me that they want and so that is what I provide. Read, watch and listen is again the mantra.

Deciding

For major decisions I follow the decision-making process that I provided earlier. For every-day decisions warm heart, cool head and a feeling this is the way forward, are my criteria. If there is any lack of clarity then I follow the FREEZE-FRAME technique referenced in the hear your heart sparkenation.

Eating

As a general rule Carol and I sit at our dining room table to eat. Another ritual is that we often prepare the meal together. We have found that a primarily plant-based diet for five days a week works for us. Further we shop for locally grown fruit and vegetables together (as well as grow our own) which are more rituals that adds to the overall experience.

Emails

My ritual is to write and reply to emails first thing in the morning and last thing before I finish work for the day. I always end the day with an empty inbox.

My clients are aware of this ritual and nobody minds.

Technology for me is a tool kit that makes my life easier and simpler. Sure I email at other times yet my ritual is only when it suits me. Technology does not control my life.

A note here about smart phones. Mine is switched off most of the time. I call people back within 24 hours. I use the phone for games and social media when it suits me. I am not on 24/7. I believe in life-work harmony as I have written about extensively in my previous works.

Events I'm hosting

I keep the twenty-four Sparkenation essentials one-sheet on my desk as a reminder that these are what I am co-creating during the event.

I open the Zoom room fifteen minutes before the start. I do my hand-on-heart ritual previously mentioned to zero in on my rhythm. I then visualise the people who will be participating and their desires and expectations.

Often I start the conversation with a group hand-on-heart experience.

Although I use the waiting room function I let people in as soon as I see they have arrived and engage in conversation.

I start all conversations on time and finish on schedule.

I use slides sparingly. My focus is on conversation. I do not do webinars or host meetings where people cannot participate live. I'm about humanisation so I will not do anything that may dehumanise.

In person is a little different. I keep people waiting outside the room. My reasoning is that unlike online they have other people to converse with. I keep the space sacred. I greet everyone at the door and make eye contact. This helps with connection later on. I have done this with thousands of people. Today my focus is small groups which makes the practice even more meaningful.

As a general rule I follow the pre and post methodologies referenced previously.

Events where I'm a participant

I want to be a model participant and be engaged. My aim is to be a person of value. As a general rule I only participate in live events. I do the occasional webinar for research.

Exercise

Carol and I walk daily, rain, hail or shine. Having dogs all of our lives has helped us to keep this ritual. We walk even when we are away from home. While walking we share out loud what we are grateful for.

We both have home exercise routines designed with us by professionals. The key is regularity. The principles of quantum leaps and the aggregation of marginal gains applies - taking small yet significants steps consistently is the pathway to everything of value in life.

Meditation

I learned breath meditation from my doctor forty-four years ago when I was looking death in the eye and I have maintained the practice!

Today I'm heart-focused and zero in on my unique rhythm several times daily, at the beginning and the end of each day, on purpose as described, and whenever I have a minute.

Podcasting

At my podcast[13] I say "no long introductions, no advertising, nothing long-winded, Podcasts for people wanting to achieve better results at less human and operating cost. Published every Friday (February - November) at 8 am Melbourne time."

You see all the rituals right? Regular and specific, exactly what the right people for me asked for.

My rituals in preparing my podcasts are also consistent and routine.

The ideas for the podcasts are percolating from helpful conversations and events. I want the topic to be current and relevant yet also to have longevity.

I start writing on Mondays and complete by Wednesday evening.

On Thursdays I record my podcasts using Zoom and the app MediaHuman Audio Converter (free) to convert Zoom file to an mp3 file.

I upload the mp3 file to Libysn, who host my podcasts, and write the copy on Thursdays. I schedule the actual release for 8 am on Fridays. I cut and paste what I have said as the associated blog post, along with resources to help you to take action.

Aside from writing which is mostly coming from my daily writing ritual, this whole process takes less than 1 hour and I'm using minimal technology at very little cost. (Zoom is less than $10 a month and Libysn around $5 per month).

Researching

Life is a research project for me. I'm always listening, noticing, observing. I'm curious and fascinated by life. I'm in awe of the wonder of every one-of-a-kind human being that I meet.

I also watch documentaries, movies, series on Netflix. I detest advertising so television is almost gone from my life. I embrace the subscription business model and pay for value.

I buy lots of books and read at least one a week. This is a ritual I have now embraced for over half my life. I tend to skim mostly these days. I make extensive notes about the ideas and concepts presented and integrate new learnings and perceptions into my own life. In the acknowledgements section of this book are my many recommended books that are in alignment with Heart-Leadership.

Silence

Often something remarkable happens following a period of silence. This has become so regular that I have come to anticipate it and look forward to it. At the same time I'm still surprised by what actually happens!

I deliberately devote parts of every day to silence. I like to sit in my garden or by a tree nearby. I like the silence in the car before an appointment and when it happens naturally during a conversation online and in person.

I have learned to trust silence and to be patient during it.

Social media

A blessing and a curse is how I describe social media. On the one hand much of it is anti-social, self-centred, self-righteous crap. It is very difficult to spot fake news and the endless disinformation and propaganda is quite simply a pain in the arse.

On the other hand there is value and insight to be given and received and the platforms can assist us in building and sustaining relationships. DC (during coronavirus) social media, I'm sure, has been helpful too many to stay in touch with family and friends.

I personally limit myself to LinkedIn, Facebook and Twitter. The latter two are always precarious. I'm on WhatsApp yet I don't see the value in always being available and so notifications for all social media are mostly switched off.

My main ritual with social media and technology platforms in general is to limit my time and energy engaging with them.

Videoing

Recently I have been uploading a short video on YouTube every Wednesday as a part of my blogging regime.

As with podcasting I record the video using Zoom. I do this on Tuesdays. Usually I upload directly to YouTube. When I have guests in my events I top and tail using iMovie before uploading direct to YouTube. Apart from the time it takes for the file to convert I'm all done in 20 minutes.

Again as with podcasting I have written what I will speak about prior and then speak direct to the camera.

Sometimes I will use the white board in my office which means taking a few minutes to set up my lighting.

As with most of my actions being a minimalist is my modis operandi. I get that some people want to do the full design studio. For me my focus is on the content and the conversation more than the technology.

Writing

I have already shared my foundational ritual to a lot of my work. I write every day. While writing this book my average has been over a thousand words per day. On one particular day while waiting for my car to be serviced I wrote 5000 words. This is the exception not the rule and it's the rule that matters.

Publishing

I have a trusted editor who has ruthlessly and lovingly read my work for over thirty years. I'm blessed that Carol has design and technological skills which I do not. Our daughter Jessica has a degree in graphic design and works in the field. We also know a successful book designer who we can hire to help us. I am particularly blessed that Carol is able to (and does so with love) meet all of the requirements for the formatting and final work that goes to Ingram Spark to ensure digital distribution and print on demand services happen flawlessly.

Post-Action Essentials

As we have learned 50% of the value to us of the actions we take happens after the action.

As you probably have guessed my go to's are after-action-reviews and integrating perception shifts and new learning with what is already going well.

Here's a refresher of my 5 stage methodology. (I use a modified version for personal actions).

1. Review one action at a time and answer the following questions What happened and why? What did we learn, relearn, and unlearn? How can we be better, wiser and more valuable in applying these learnings? Who will we become? What will we do next?

2. Determine with your colleagues how your answers will be integrated with what is already working well for you.

3. Upgrade your individual, team and organisational plans and co-promises on a page accordingly.

4. Reflect new perceptions in appropriate standard operating procedures, policies and practices.

5. Upgrade learning and development materials.

When it comes to professional matters, wherever possible, I include Performance Possibility Partners and Performance Possibility Peers in stages 1 and 2.

Turning Possibility Into Reality - further suggested actions

- I trust that you have been contemplating your own pre action rituals and post action essentials and have begun to determine your own. Now is the time to write them down and clarify them.

- Share what you decide with Possibility Peers and Possibility Partners individually and in your peer groups.

- Undertake a focus audit by detailing everything you do for the next month. Reflect on where your time and energy is going and then change/modify/nuance your actions. My own methodology is to determine regularly what I will Keep, Cease, and Begin in order to sustain a methodology for perpetual renaissance in my life and work.

Do Your Work.

Notes

1 https://www.ianberry.biz/reasons-relationships-routines-guarantee-results/

2 https://youtu.be/SM1ckkGwqZI

3 https://www.kotterinc.com/8-steps-process-for-leading-change/

4 https://www.davidcooperrider.com/ai-process/

5 https://jamesclear.com/marginal-gains

6 https://www.ianberry.biz/sustaining-shared-view/

7 https://www.ianberry.biz/21st-century-leadership-books/

8 https://www.creativityincbook.com/catmull/

9 https://www.compassionatemind.org.au/compassion

10 https://www.ianberry.biz/wp-content/uploads/2020/03/CompellingConversationGaryEdwardsIanBerry2.pdf

11 https://www.ianberry.biz/heart-leadership-village/

12 https://www.progressprinciple.com/

13 https://ianberrypodcasts.libsyn.com/

Sparkenation Five

Happenstance is a consequence of harmony, heart, head, and hands

"The privilege of a lifetime is being who you are."
Joseph Campbell

Overview

Our present and our future as Heart-Leaders is determined in four ways:

- Being in harmony with ourselves, other people and our environment.
- What we feel and hear in our hearts.
- What we make of it in our heads and the decisions and choices we make.
- How we give these feelings, thoughts, decisions and choices life through the actions we take with our hands.

One result of this meaningful work is happenstance.

On all the many trips I have made to London, my usual ritual is to catch the Paddington Express from Heathrow to Paddington Station and make my way to my first destination from there.

On one occasion I took a wrong turn on the way out of Heathrow and immediately bumped into a client of mine from Australia whose circumstances had been weighing on my heart on the plane.

This is happenstance.

The more we stay in harmony, hear our hearts, ask our heads and engage our hands, the more happenstance happens.

You might call this synchronicity, which the famous psychologist Carl Jung introduced as a concept. He meant meaningful coincidences.

You may call what I am describing here serendipity.

I chose happenstance because I wanted something starting with H to be my mnemonic as well as an aid for you in applying the Heart-Leadership principles herein in your own best way.

I wish you well as you sustain harmony, hear your heart, ask your head, and engage your hands.

Harmony, Heart, Head, Hands in this order lead to coherence which in turn leads to Happenstance.

"Coherence is the state when the heart, mind and emotions are in energetic alignment and cooperation," HeartMath Institute Research Director Dr. Rollin McCraty says. *"It is a state that builds resiliency – personal energy is accumulated, not wasted – leaving more energy to manifest intentions and harmonious outcomes."*[1]

Also from HeartMath:

"When the physiological coherence mode is driven by a positive emotional state, we call it psychophysiological coherence. This state is associated with sustained positive emotion and a high degree of mental and emotional stability.

"In states of psychophysiological coherence, there is increased synchronization and harmony between the cognitive, emotional and physiological systems, resulting in efficient and harmonious functioning of the whole. ... Studies conducted across diverse

populations have linked the capacity to self-generate and sustain psychophysiologically coherent states at will with numerous benefits."[2]

In my own experience I have learned that our hearts know the present and the future whereas our heads only know the past.

It has taken a lot of personal work to get my head to be quiet and to only ask it when I am ready for the how to's. I'm realising that this is a key to my own coherence.

I believe such coherence is vital to being who we are and this, as Joseph Campbell reminded us, is the privilege of a lifetime.

Turning Possibility Into Reality - further suggested actions

- Begin to notice instances of happenstance/synchronicity/serendipity in your life and work. Create a journal and record the patterns you notice.

- What nuances will you make to increase the likelihood of coherence in your life?

- Share your insights, inspirations and ideas about coherence and happenstance with Possibility Peers and Possibility Partners individually and in your peer groups.

- Be grateful for happenstance before, during and after it occurs.

Do Your Work.

Notes

1 https://www.heartmath.org/articles-of-the-heart/the-math-of-heartmath/coherence/

2 https://www.heartmath.org/articles-of-the-heart/the-math-of-heartmath/coherence/

Epilogue

To sustain being in harmony with yourself, other people, and our planet, and then to consistently hear your heart first, ask your head second, engage your hands third, takes a lot of deliberate practice before it becomes habitual.

I share some of my own story below and that of Carol's to encourage you to stay your course no matter what.

"The only thing that keeps us down and keeps us stuck is our thoughts." said the Canadian writer John Kehoe.

Reading John's insight in 1990 was a game changer for me.

My heart was telling me then that I should leave the corporate world and begin self-employment.

I felt my heart calling me to be more than I was and to do work that I felt could better serve people.

My head was filled with doubts and worry and thoughts that I was putting my family at risk if it didn't work out.

The expressions 'doing my head in' and 'weighing heavily on my mind' had a lot of traction.

I followed my heart yet I was full of fear.

Fast-forward 30 years and I am still following my heart. There's been highs and lows and lots in between.

There have been times when I allowed my head to overrule my heart. The consequences were never good.

There have been times when I followed my heart, only to allow myself to be overcome with doubt and worry and quit too soon. Equally allowing my head to rule has also meant hanging onto things for way too long.

Always my life has been better when I have followed my heart, kept a cool head, engaged my hands and moved forward one small yet significant step (quantum leap) at a time.

My deepest insights into to the matters of, and the preeminence of the heart, began on September 15th 2017. Carol received the exciting news, on this day, of her registration as a civil celebrant.

On the same day she received the news after many tests that she had cancer of an unknown primary (about 30% of cancers) that had metastasised in lymph nodes in her neck and chest cavity.

Carol's prognosis wasn't good and she began chemotherapy almost immediately.

In the next five months she lost her energy, her hair and almost her life.

I became her primary carer. To say that our lives were changed forever doesn't do justice to what happened.

A few days after her first chemo treatment, which involved five long hours sitting while being injected with toxic drugs, we were in our lounge room watching TV.

I happened to glance at Carol only to see her eyes rolling and her losing consciousness. I called the hospital emergency number given to us and there was no answer. I then called the ambulance emergency line to be told by the operator to slap Carol hoping to wake her and then to keep her awake until the ambulance arrived.

I followed instructions and with great fear experienced the longest nineteen minutes of my life with Carol barely conscious when the ambulance officers entered our home.

After connecting Carol to machines and getting her to stand her blood pressure dropped 30 points and they explained to me that they would give her some drugs to stabilise her and then take her to hospital.

As they wheeled her to the ambulance I burst into tears and felt an acute loss of energy only to be reassured that everything would be fine.

A hour later, when I got to see Carol in the emergency ward, she had recovered quite a bit. It was explained to me that she had had a severe reaction to the chemo drugs and required a hospital stay for a few days to recover.

We learned over the next few months that Western doctors know a lot about chemicals and trauma recovery yet, we learned the hard way, they know very little (with few exceptions) about human energy and human well-being.

Carol decided that she would take charge of her own recovery and got well primarily through her own resilience. She enhanced her gift of being able to learn about all the options and chose what resonated with her heart.

In essence, over time, Carol changed her energy vibration/frequency with the help of changed diet, exercise regime, and the use of sound waves and frequencies through rife and scalar machines.

She also learned to hear her hearts connection to the present and future and pay less attention to her head's connection to the past.

Of course I benefited greatly from the numerous conversations we had and continue to have. I participated too in the changes Carol was making in my own best way.

These conversations, observations and changes prepared me well for my own cancer battle and enabled me to change my energy vibration/frequency as well.

Only being able to work part time during the peak of Carol's journey meant I had to reinvent my professional practice.

Such reinvention is not new to me as I have deliberately reinvented myself most years since I began my work in leadership development in 1990.

What was new this time was the drugs I now had to take to keep my melanoma at bay.

Beginning in November 2018 the first drug knocked me around significantly, in particular regarding my energy levels. I experienced chronic fatigue for the first time.

In January 2020 I changed to a different drug, experiencing similar side affects including liver and kidney inflammation and a rash all over my body which, at one point, was almost unbearable.

In May 2020 I began taking a third drug with the promise of minimal side affects. After initial challenges getting the dosage right I am now coping well.

In order to sustain my well-being and do my best work I have chosen to work significantly reduced hours - about a quarter of the time I once worked. Interestingly I am as productive as I have ever been. I'm enjoying my work more than ever too.

An evolution of models

I'm a strong believer in metaphors, models and methodologies because my experience tells me that they help immensely in keeping us grounded as we follow our hearts, ask our heads and engage our hands.

In the late 1990's, a time some writers have noted as the beginning of another renaissance[1], I observed that values and value based businesses were on the rise.

I saw this accelerate over the next decade. Much of my work into the 2000's was helping my clients to live their values and deliver value.

A consequence of client work and conversations with clients was the realisation that people need to feel genuinely valued before they will consistently live values and deliver remarkable value.

The concept of people feeling valued, living values and delivering value became the trademark of my work.

By 2014 my feelings and thoughts evolved to the model pictured below.

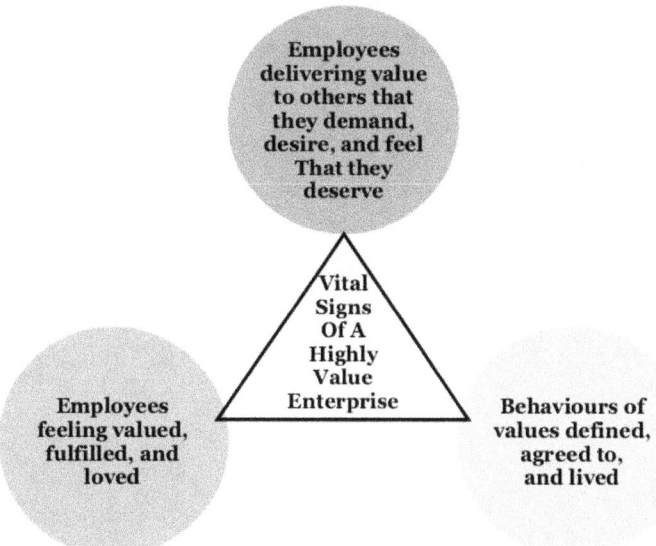

In 2015 and 2016 I worked intensively once a month with a peer group of my clients and this culminated in 'The Appreciative Leader' publication[2]. Central to the work was the following evolution of the previous model:

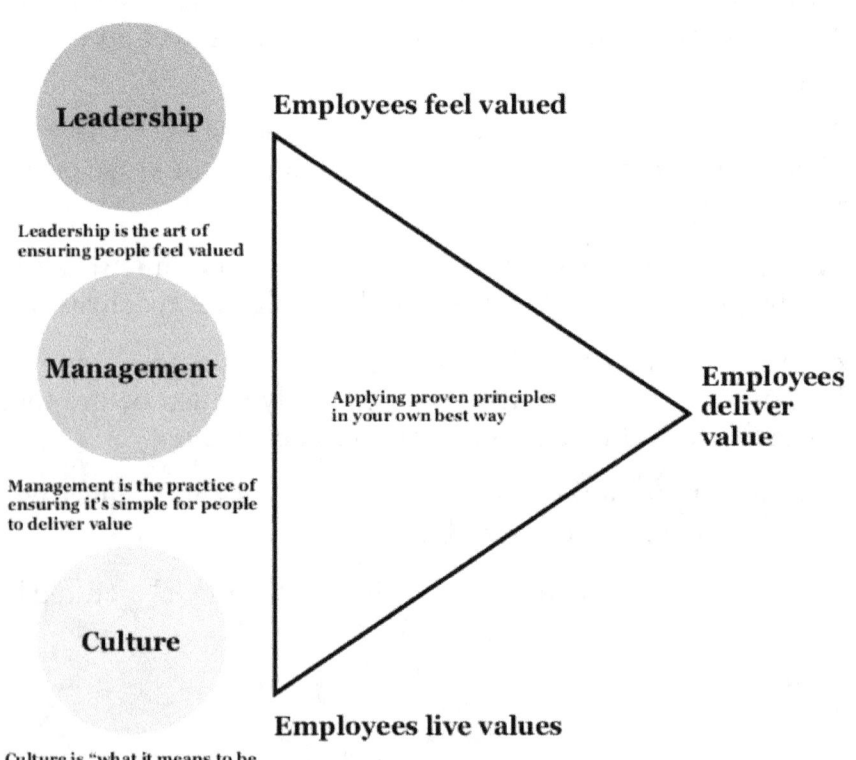

In 2018 and the first half of 2019 I again worked with a peer group of my clients. That work culminated in the 'Remarkable Workplaces' workbook[3].

Central to the work was the following evolution of the main model:

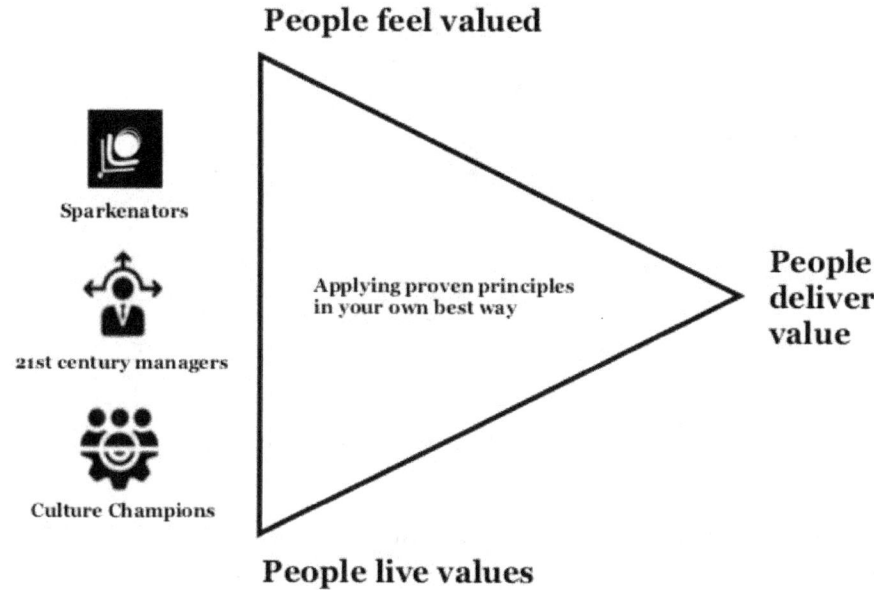

I knew in my heart and head that further evolution was necessary.

I invested many hours in heart-based meditation and contemplation and conversation with clients before arriving at the next model which I workshopped with Jamie Wilson and his team in December 2019.

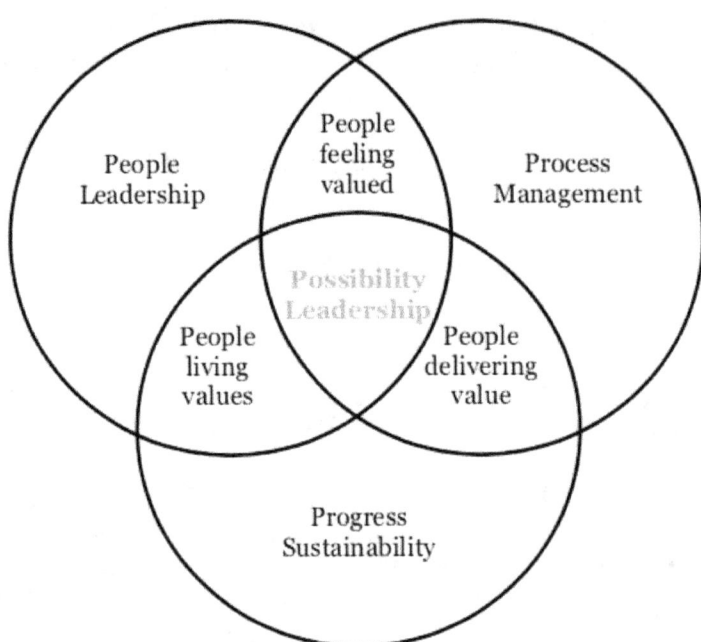

Jamie was a highly valued member of both the peer groups mentioned above.

Following Jamie's workshop he and I had a conversation that confirmed a feeling in my heart that it was Heart-Leadership at the centre not Possibility Leadership.

I confirmed this feeling further when I ran a short series of online workshops with selected clients in January and February 2020.

Many comments in the forums and global online gatherings of The Right Company[4], further confirmed what my heart was telling me.

In addition, happenstance led me to reconnect with a colleague based in the UAE, Susan Furness, in February 2020. We rapidly created a new program together which we called Strategic Heartistry[5]. Susan now leads this program.

My work with Susan further validated and contributed to my sense that Heart-Leadership was my work for the foreseeable future.

The model evolution central to this book was workshopped with a select group of wonderful people in August 2020. These folk are acknowledged in the next section.

Epilogue

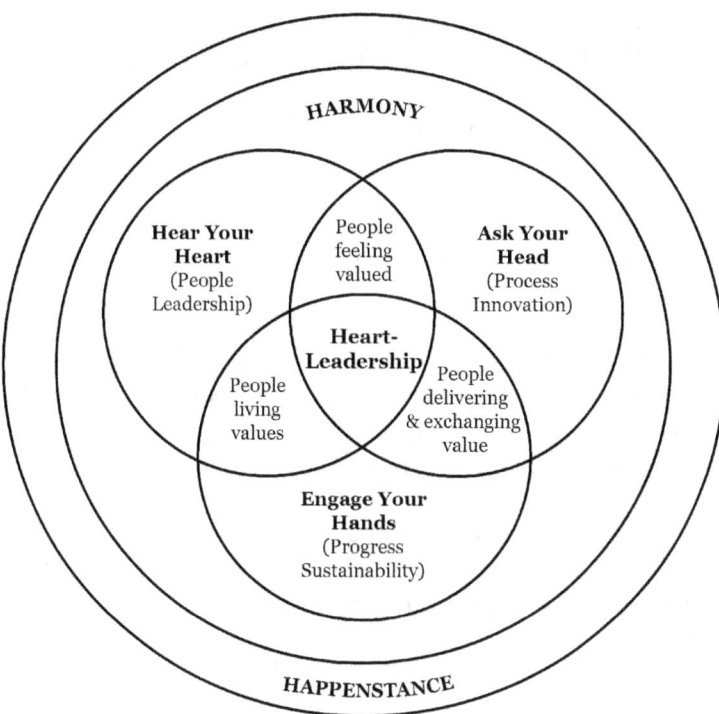

Here's what a member of my Heart-Leadership Online Village, Laura Potter says about her Heart-Leadership journey:

"I've often been confused between what my heart or head are telling me. I find that if I think too long, beyond my initial feelings, the process can get muddled.

I've recently moved into a senior leadership role and I do think being in tune with your heart and head is critical.

As a leader there are daily decisions to make, and you are more closely judged by what you do or do not do, and how you do it, so it becomes crucial to act with integrity, so you can back yourself.

I recently learned about head, heart, hand from Ian. It resonated with me, I pondered it for days, and I noticed that as I approached difficult decisions, some which would have significant impact on others like recruitment choices, team direction, giving honest feedback, I started putting my hand over my heart. What was it telling me, truly? What was my instinct telling me?

I often feel that we hear that little voice, telling us something isn't right, or to not walk down a particular road, or to re-check a locked door, but we often ignore it, and I would bet most of you have experienced moments where you wish you could rewind and listen to that voice and have acted on it.

Which is why I find myself starting with my heart. I'm becoming better at listening to it, feeling it, stopping for a moment and tuning in.

I'm enjoying the process of taking in heart-felt insight, applying some practical thinking to it (the head), and backing myself in moving forward (the hand). I may not always get it right, but I do feel more confident in myself and my decisions."

Laura took to Heart-Leadership quickly beginning only in August 2020. Like me however, and I suspect you, seeing you have made it this far, the journey actually began long ago.

Laura has simply, yet profoundly, chosen to become the wise leader she wants to be.

Who will you become? What will you do next?

In becoming the wise leader you want to be I suggest you choose one insight that your heart is telling you, in this moment, is right for you.

Sit with what you hear your heart saying maybe for a day or two. Then take your time in deciding what your next small yet significant steps (quantum leaps) will be to move from where you are to your next reality.

> *"Are you in earnest? Seize this very minute:*
>
> *What you can do, or dream you can, begin it;*
>
> *Boldness has genius, power, and magic in it."*
>
> **Johann Wolfgang von Goethe.**

Epilogue

Maybe I can help you

I work with a handful of clients at any given time. Let's have a conversation. Please telephone me on +61 418 807 898 in business hours AEST or text me with three possible times to call you and I will do so within 24 hours.

How we may be able to work together is overviewed at https://www.ianberry.biz/heart-leadership/

I wish you every success as a Heart-Leader as you enhance energy, hold it when required, and shift it whenever appropriate.

Notes

1 Age Of Discovery, Bloomsbury, 2016, Ian Goldin and Chris Kutarna.

2 https://www.ianberry.biz/appreciative-leader-handbook-ian-berry/

3 https://www.ianberry.biz/remarkable-workplaces/

4 https://therightcompany.co/

5 https://strategicheartistry.com/

Acknowledgements

I'm very grateful to participants in the inaugural Heart-Leadership Peer Group Program who in workshopping the working draft of this book helped me to nuance and crystallise my feelings, thoughts and actions. Big thank you to Jacquie Landeman, Laura Potter, Simone Boer, Brad Gray, Donovan Ryan, Paul Schmeja, Jamie Wilson and Jody Tucker.

I'm also grateful to the above and to the following people for reading the working draft and offering suggestions - Peter Acheson, Glenn Capelli, Rosemary Ferguson-McKenzie, Susan Furness, Robyn Henderson, Peter Hills, John Kennedy, Geoff McDonald, Leanne Perryman, David Sproules.

Special thanks to Alistair Rego, Strategic Solutions/Media Solutions Alumni for gifting Susan Furness and myself a phrase during our Strategic Heartistry co-creation, *"Being decisively human in a digitally connected world."* This phrase greatly influenced my version - Being Decisively Human in a Decidedly Digital World.

My heartfelt thanks to Ann Blair who has edited my writings for over 30 years and who has also worked with a number of my clients as a mentor.

Special thanks to my daughter Jessica for the cover design and creation of the new Heart-Leadership logo.

And to Carol for conversations, suggestions, book layout and taking care of all things publishing with skill and commitment, and especially love.

Books I recommend

The following authors and their books stirred my heart, challenged my head, and inspired my hands to take action in a decisively human way:

Twilight of Democracy The Failure of Politics and The Parting Of Friends, Penguin Books, Anne Applebaum.

Human kind A Hopeful History, Bloomsbury, 2020, Rutger Bregman.

Daring Greatly. How the Courage to Be Vulnerable Transforms the Way We Live, Love, Parent and Lead, Penguin 2012, Brene Brown.

The Hero with a Thousand Faces, Pantheon Books, 1949, Joseph Campbell

Thinking Caps, Capa Pty Ltd, 2009, Glenn Capelli.

Finite and Infinite Games, Free Press, 1986 James P.Carse.

Everybody Matters The Extraordinary Power of Caring for Your People Like Family, Portfolio Penguin, 2015, Bob Chapman and Raj Sisodia.

Atomic Habits Tiny Changes, Remarkable Results, Random House Business Books, 2018, James Clear.

The HeartMath Solution, HarperCollins e-books, 1999, Doc Childre and Howard Martin with Donna Beech.

Humans Are Underrated, Portfolio / Penguin, 2015, Geoff Colvin.

The 8th Habit, Free Press, 2004, Stephen R. Covey.

The 3rd Alternative, Simon & Shuster, 2011, Stephen R. Covey with Breck England.

Brave New Work, Portfolio Penguin, 2019, Aaron Dignan.

Illuminate: Ignite Change with Speeches, Stories, Ceremonies, and Symbols, Portfolio Books, 2016, Nancy Duarte and Patti Sanchez.

Resonate: present visual stories that transform audiences, John Wiley & Sons, 2010, Nancy Duarte.

The Power of Habit - why we do what we do and how to change, Random House Publishers, 2013, Charles T. Duhigg.

Mindset: The New Psychology of Success, Random House, 2007, Carol S. Dweck.

You'll See It When You Believe It, Arrow, 1990, Wayne Dyer.

The More Beautiful World Our Hearts Know is Possible, North Atlantic Books, 2013, Charles Eisenstein.

The Power of Unreasonable People, Harvard Business Press, 2008, John Elkington and Pamela Hartigan.

The Radical Leap, Dearborn Trade Publishing, 2004, Steve Farber.

Love is Just Damn Good Business: Do What You Love in the Service of People Who Love What You Do, McGraw-Hill Education, 2019, Steve Farber.

The Power of Kindness, Penguin 2006, Piero Ferrucci.

Don't Be Evil, The Case Against Big Tech, Penguin Books, Rana Foroohar.

How to Lead a Quest, John Wiley & Son Australia, 2016, Dr. Jason Fox.

The Game Changer, John Wiley & Son Australia, 2014, Dr. Jason Fox.

Man's Search For Meaning, Beacon Press, 2006 (original publication) 1946, Victor Frankl.

The Checklist Manifesto How To Get Things Right, Profile Books Ltd, 2010, Atul Gawande.

Purple Cow, Portfolio, a member of Penguin Group, 2003, Seth Godin.

Age Of Discovery, Bloomsbury, 2016, Ian Goldin and Chris Kutarna.

What Got You Here Won't Get You There, Hyperion, 2007, Marshall Goldsmith.

The God Argument: The Case against Religion and for Humanism, Bloomsbury, 2013, A. C. Grayling.

The Age of Genius The Seventeenth Century & The Birth of The Modern Mind, Bloomsbury, 2016, A. C. Grayling.

Humanocracy : creating organizations as amazing as the people inside them, Harvard Business School Publishing, 2020, Gary Hamel and Michele Zanini.

The Hungry Spirit, Hutchinson, 1997, Charles Handy.

Sapiens: A Brief History of Humankind, Vintage, 2015, Yuval Noah Harari.

Homo Deus: A Brief History of Tomorrow, Vintage, 2017, Yuval Noah Harari.

21 Lessons for the 21st Century, Vintage, 2018, Yuval Noah Harari.

Lost Connections, Bloomsbury, 2018, Johann Hari.

Willful Blindness, Simon & Shuster, 2011, Margaret Heffernan.

The Art of Happiness, Hodder & Stoughton, 1998, His Holiness the Dalai Lama and Howard C. Culter, M.D.

Stillness is the key, Profile Books, 2019, Ryan Holiday.

The Purpose Economy, Elevate Publishing, 2016, Aaron Hurst.

Story Driven - You Don't Need To Compete When You Know Who You Are, Perceptive Press, 2019, Bernadette Jiwa.

Reinventing organisations, Nelson Parker, 2014, Frederice Laloux.

Technology vs. Humanity The coming clash between man and machine, Fast Future Publishing Ltd 2016, Gerd Leonhard.

Essentialism The Disciplined Pursuit of Less, Virgin Books, 2014, Greg McKeown,

Rebalancing Society, Berrett-Koehler Publishers, Inc, 2015, Henry Mintzberg.

Out of the Wreckage A New Politics for an Age of Crisis, Verso, 2017, George Monbiot.

Metaskills: Five Talents For The Robotic Age, New Rider, 2013, Marty Neumeier.

Deep Work: Rules for Focused Success in a Distracted World, Grand Central Publishing, 2016, Cal Newport.

Acknowledgements

Local Is Our Future, Local Futures, 2019, Helena Norber-Hodge.

The Heart of Success, Hodder & Stoughton, 2002, Rob Parsons.

The Excellence Dividend Principles for Prospering in Turbulent Times from a Lifetime in Pursuit of Excellence, Nicholas Brealey Publishing, 2018, Tom Peters.

Drive – the surprising truth about what motivate us, Canongate, 2010, Daniel Pink.

Doughnut Economics Seven Ways to Think Like a 21st Century Economist, rh business books, 2017, Kate Raworth.

Lovemarks the future beyond brands, Murdoch Books, 2004, Kevin Roberts.

The Element, Penguin Books, 2009, Ken Robinson.

Team Human, W. W. Norton & Company, 2019, Douglas Rushkoff.

the untethered soul, New Harbinger Publications Inc, 2007, Michael Singer.

Start With Why, Portfolio, a member of Penguin Group (USA) Inc. 2009, Simon Sinek.

The Infinite Game, Penguin Books Ltd, 2019, Simon Sinek.

Another Now, dispatches from an alternative present, The Body Head London, Yanis Varoufakis.

Making Sense of the Organization, John Wiley & Sons, 2000, Karl E. Weick.

Turning to One Another: Simple Conversations to Restore Hope to the Future, Berrett-Koehler Publishers, Inc. 2009, Margaret J. Wheatley.

Sand Talk: How Indigenous Thinking Can Save the World, Text Publishing, 2019, Tyson Yunkaporta.

Additional Resources

There's videos, podcasts and online courses via this page https://www.ianberry.biz/heart-leadership-resources/

For my latest work please visit https://blog.ianberry.biz/

> *"And now here is my secret, a very simple secret,*
> *it is only with the heart that one can see rightly;*
> *what is essential is invisible to the eye."*
>
> **Antoine de Saint-Exupéry**

About Ian

For over 30 years I've been working with leaders to stay ahead of the curve in the world of work. Leaders in privately owned and family businesses, proven purpose driven organisations and corporations, professional service firms, and solo professional service providers.

I've had the privilege of working with more than 1,000 leaders, women and men, in over forty countries.

Leaders like Darren[1] who was faced with significant challenges and following a review asked for my help. Five years on Darren's business is thriving. We are still working together.

My essence is to sense what most people don't, say what I sense in inspirational ways, and to shine lights on what's possible for you, and then help you to turn possibility into reality.

From 1974 - 1990 I enjoyed a very successful corporate finance career including leading a 100 million dollar business unit.

I held Branch, Regional, and State manager roles in three Australian states receiving numerous awards for my leadership, development of people, and results.

I'm a pioneer in the development and use of one-page plans and many associated innovations such as one-sentence strategy and one-quantum leap at a time momentum.

As a Professional Speaker I've given more than 3,000 presentations (700+ keynotes and 2,300+ presentation/conversations (over 500 online) from thirty minutes to three to four hours to one day).

I'm a Past National President of the Professional Speakers Association of Australia.

The time, energy and money you invest in people development and business process improvement should yield you the greatest return of all your investments. I'm here for you to help you make this possibility a reality.

---

[1] https://www.ianberry.biz/what-people-say/

www.ingramcontent.com/pod-product-compliance
Lightning Source LLC
Chambersburg PA
CBHW051947290426
44110CB00015B/2149